SECRETS
TO
WEDDING DRESS
SHOPPING

AN INSIDER'S GUIDE TO
SAYING YES TO YOUR DRESS
FROM
COLORADO'S WEDDING DRESS EXPERTS

BY
MINDI & JORDAN LINSCOMBE
OWNERS OF SOMETHING NEW BOUTIQUE
COLORADO SPRINGS, COLORADO
AND
HEATHER & JIM BUTLER

DEDICATION:
MINDI

I'm full of gratitude to my Savior Jesus Christ for giving me the strength to work hard and dream big. I dedicate the book to my dear husband Jordan, our sons, our family, the SNB team, and the thousands of brides & customers we've had the privilege to serve!

JORDAN

In gratefulness for what Jesus Christ has done for me, I dedicate this to my wonderful wife Mindi, our boys, our family, and my late grandfather Oran—who took risks in business and left a legacy.

This publication is designed to provide accurate and authoritative information in regard to the subject matter covered. It is sold with the understanding that the publisher is not engaged in rendering legal, accounting, or other professional service. If legal advice or other expert assistance is required, the services of a professional should be sought.

Linscombe, Mindi and Jordan & Butler, Heather and Jim
Secrets to Wedding Dress Shopping: An Insider's Guide to Saying Yes to Your Dress from Colorado's Wedding Dress Experts
ISBN: 978-1505321401
  1. Fashion

What Others Are Saying About
Secrets to Wedding Dress Shopping

"Something New Boutique has made the dress finding process not only simple but the most enjoyable experience. Where the girl truly comes before the dress, customer service is our #1 priority and the professionalism is top notch. One of the best bridal stores in the country."- Kelsi Cole

"This book is such a stress-reliever because it tells you what you need to know before shopping! A go-to guide and must-have for ALL brides!" - Alexandra Carlson

I wish I had a place like Something New Boutique and Mindi's insight's from this book to help me when I was shopping for my wedding dress! - Catherine Beeler

"I love this book! It's the ideal guide to making those big decisions in ways you won't regret! I SO wish I had this when I was planning my wedding!" - Alyssa Luckey

"This book is a great resource to have for all the questions that may arrive when looking for my wedding dress!" - Kayla Knight

CONTENTS

INTRODUCTION

Hi, we're Mindi and Jordan Linscombe of Something New Boutique in Colorado Springs, Colorado.

We're so excited by your recent engagement and thank you for purchasing a copy of our book, *Secrets to Wedding Dress Shopping*. We have written this book to help you find the perfect wedding gown as you plan your wedding. We think you'll find this book will save you a lot of time and money and will be one of the best resources you'll be able to turn to again and again as you prepare for the wedding of your dreams.

We're excited to share with you in this introduction some things that are unique to Colorado that you should carefully consider before buying your gown.

Here at Something New Boutique, you'll have a world-class experience dealing with our professional bridal consultants. Our friendly and courteous bridal consultants are true specialists and are ready to help you as you plan all of the important details for your big day. Our goal is to simply take the guesswork out of planning everything you'll wear on your big day.

You'll notice the difference from the minute you step into our beautiful store. You'll be greeted warmly by one of our professional and courteous bridal specialists and assisted in completing a simple bridal registry form. This will help the bridal specialist get a sense for your personal style and the ideas you've already put together for your wedding plans. She'll be able to help you try on the different silhouettes and help you find only the best one for you!

As a bride in Colorado, we want you to know that we have helped thousands of brides get married in all sorts of venues all across the region. The venue you choose will have special meaning to you and your guests and we look forward to helping you dress your best for your special day! You'll find very helpful information in this book, regardless of your chosen venue that will help you plan and consider all of the aspects of finding the perfect dress and how that decision will influence the many other options you have as you plan for your wedding.

At our store, there are seven specific things you'll discover that you won't find anywhere else. Here are several specific things you'll discover at our store:

1. **You'll enjoy an incredible selection of gowns that you won't find anywhere else in the state of Colorado.**

We design our own exclusive dresses at our store and our brides tell us that the dresses they find here are not only unique, but are truly on the cutting edge of fashion.

The chapters we've written on "Myths of Wedding Dress Shopping" and "The 10 Commandments of Shopping for a Dress" are real eye openers and will help you discover the things you must know before you buy your dress. Once you read these chapters, you'll know exactly what you must do to showcase your unique style and personality in a stunning dress that will draw every eye to you and the gown you've chosen throughout your big day!

2. **With our huge selection of hundreds of gowns, sizes 0-28, you'll be able to try on your gown in your size.**

Shopping at Something New Boutique is the same as going to several other smaller stores who just don't have the extensive inventory that we do. Make sure you read the chapter we've written on "Shapes, Silhouettes, and Styles" as it will give you some helpful tips on which gown style will fit you best. This chapter along with the chapters on necklines and trains will help you prepare for your bridal gown appointment at our store. At Something New, we have taken special care to bring a wide variety of all four silhouettes to you, so you'll be able to find the perfect dress that will help you create the dream you've been planning for so long.

3. **Every gown purchased at Something New Boutique goes through our proprietary 5-Point Premium Care Treatment process. So,**

whether you purchase your gown from our in-stock selection or special order your gown, you are assured of an absolutely stunning wedding gown that will be exquisitely prepared for your wedding day.

Our 5-Point Premium Care Treatment begins with the inspection of the gown you've chosen. Our specialists carefully examine every aspect of the dress, including its exquisite ornamentation to ensure that everything is in place and in impeccable condition. Then, we press / steam your dress so it is wrinkle free and lays perfectly on your figure. Many stores do not steam or press the gown when it arrives. Here at Something New Boutique, we look over every inch of your gown and ensure that it is ready for your wedding with the same degree of care and precision that we would if it was our own daughter's wedding dress. No other store in Colorado provides the same level of treatment and care that we do for the wedding gowns we sell at our store.

4. **Something New Boutique is one of the most highly recommended, locally owned bridal salons in all of Colorado.**

In fact, we have personally assisted thousands of brides over the years at our store. Our brides love how we have cared for them and helped them prepare for their wedding day. Over the years, we have received countless thank you notes from brides and their mothers who have entrusted their wedding experiences to our store and staff. You can hear many of these comments from brides on our web site at www.somethingnewboutique.com.

More than 60% of the brides who buy from us do so because they've been referred by one of their friends or family who have also had a great experience at our store. We share this with you because we want you to know that you're in great hands at our store. Our customer service goes beyond mere words. We promise to do our utmost in helping you with all of your bridal attire needs. We'll handle all of the details for you so you won't have to worry or be stressed as you navigate your way through the many decisions you'll make in preparation for one of the most exciting days of your life!

5. **When you arrive at our store, you'll find several great savings options that you'll receive when you purchase your dress at your first visit to our store and after you purchase your dress. We also have a FREE gift waiting for you that you have to see to believe!**

In addition, you'll receive four exclusive coupons available ONLY to our customers that will allow you to save BIG money on jewelry, bridesmaids dresses, tuxedo rentals, and your wedding gown preservation. Your caring bridal consultant will be able to explain how she can help you save money on your first visit to our store when you arrive to fill out a bridal registry form with her.

6. **Our unique, stylish bridesmaid dresses are available in over 65 colors that even your pickiest bridesmaid will LOVE!**

The chapter you'll read on Dressing the Bridesmaids, will give you lots of great tips and ideas to help make this one of the most rewarding and least stressful experiences in your wedding shopping! In fact, this entire book you are reading will become indispensable to you as you go shopping for all your wedding needs.

7. **Our brides can get back every penny of the money they've spent on their wedding gown (minus the sales tax) up to one year from purchase date with our easy referral program.**

Something New brides get an unbelievable array of coupons and special pricing reserved only for our brides from some of the top wedding vendors in all of Colorado. Your wedding guests will all wonder when you come down the aisle, "How could she afford a dress like that?" and you'll be able to smile and know that you saved a bundle by buying your dress from Something New Boutique.

Over the years our brides tell us they're surprised at how easy it is to afford our unparalleled world-class quality gowns. Our goal at our store is to make the process of getting your wedding gown easy, stress-free, and without any of the high pressure you might experience at other salons. But you don't have to take their word for it, find out for yourself! We're confident you'll say the same and know you'll be delighted when you visit us at our store!

We hope you enjoy the book we've put together. There are big secrets that you'll find within these pages that will help you save money, be better prepared, and enjoy the experience of getting married even more. We can't wait to meet you at our store and look forward to helping you find the perfect wedding dress!

Mindi and Jordan Linscombe

P.S. You can receive a special coupon we've created just for you that you can use at our store on your first visit by emailing us at: info@somethingnewboutique.com. You can schedule an appointment at our store by visiting our web site or by calling us at **(719) 282-6500**. When you call in, we'll give you a special access code so you can activate the savings of our First Visit Advantage Program with the purchase of your gown which will save you up to $300 on your total purchase with us. You're going to love your experience at Something New Boutique. We can't wait to have you in our store and help you prepare for one of the most meaningful and special days of your life!

Section 1:
Your Wedding

The 9 Most Common Mistakes Couples Make Following Engagement and What to Do About Them

Congratulations on your recent engagement! As you're enjoying the glow and excitement of your new commitment to each other, consider the nine most common mistakes made by recently engaged couples. Make your plans for the perfect wedding while minimizing your stress, frustration, and disappointment.

1. Not taking the time to envision the details of your wedding.
When will the big day happen? Where should it be? Who will be there? How formal will the event be? What are the prior commitments of loved ones, friends, and the availability of the location and vendors desired? It is your wedding so take time now to think through the details. Many couples today are waiting longer to get married, but aren't taking enough time to think through all of the details (so they're more stressed out and end up settling for things instead of getting just what they want). Don't let this happen to you. To have the wedding of your dreams, a lot of thought and planning are required, yet fortunately, there are professionals who can help you think through things you may not have considered (since they help couples plan their weddings all of the time). At Something New Boutique, we can introduce you to wedding vendors that can help you plan a wedding day you'll always treasure and no one will ever forget.

2. Neglecting to decide on a budget and keeping track of your expenditures.
Very few people like budgets or budgeting, but not having one can add a significant burden to your present and future financial situation. There are literally endless options to a wedding and, unfortunately, how elaborate

many of the details are comes down to how much money you are willing to spend (the average wedding in America costs around $19,581). Your budget may fluctuate as you decide on the actual venue and find out who has committed to help you cover the costs, but it is critical that you begin with a dollar amount in mind.

3.   Forgetting to create a wedding timeline and taking action on the details. A common mistake made by many couples is that they wait too long before taking action on important details for their wedding. To receive a free planning calendar for your wedding, come by Something New Boutique today. In addition, there are other checklists you can get at our store that will detail the responsibilities of each member of your wedding party before, during and after the wedding. These checklists are very helpful and countless brides have expressed their gratitude to having these lists so easily accessible. With this calendar or date book, you can set specific dates by which you want to get things accomplished.

4. Waiting too long to order your wedding dress or bridesmaid dresses.
Bride's magazine recommends that you purchase your wedding gown at least a year before your wedding. Determine what you are looking for early. For a one of a kind experience you'll never forget where you'll get the attention and service you deserve (and receive a free gift upon arriving), call **(719) 282-6500** to schedule an appointment. You'll be glad you did.

5. Trying to do it alone.
Create a timeline, divide up the planning, and assign tasks that need to be completed. Both of you should be involved in the planning of the wedding. Your mother and bridesmaids can also offer invaluable assistance in the planning. Once a task has been completed, check it off so you don't end up doing the same thing twice! We have also put together opportunities for you and your fiancé to meet with many local wedding vendors so you can get help from helpful professionals who care as much about your wedding as you do. Check with our store for the next event you could attend to get some help with planning out all of the details for your wedding.

6. Assuming the wedding will just work itself out and not scheduling enough time to work on your wedding details.
Many brides find it very helpful to set up a specific day of the week when they'll focus on their wedding plans. If your engagement is not as long, you may want to spend a couple of days each week or plan several weekends where you can focus on what needs to be done. Staying organized and communicating effectively are essential to staying sane and getting it all done.

7. Forgetting how many people you can accommodate at your reception site.
As you put together your guest list, think about how many people you'll be able to accommodate for your ceremony and reception site. Your food and beverage budget may also be a factor in who you invite since more guests often means more money.

8. Waiting too long to choose bridesmaids and groomsmen.
The earlier you decide and ask, the more time you'll have to let them help you plan the details of your wedding. Think through and pick who you will choose to honor as your attendants. Choose individuals who have been your friends through thick and thin and who you'll enjoy spending time with as you plan and prepare. It is a good idea to let them know what will be involved and expected, since many of them will be contributing their precious time (helping to plan the details) and hard-earned money (purchasing gowns, renting tuxedos, etc.). They'll be honored by your request and your friendship will grow deeper as they participate in your special day.

9. Forgetting to take time to relax.
If you find yourself getting stressed out, take some time to recuperate. Spend a day completely away from the planning. Have fun. Relax. Enjoy spending time with your fiancé. Create special moments that will deepen and enhance your relationship. Forgetting to focus on what is important will cause you a lot more stress than it is worth. Don't feel like you have to do everything in one day. Pace yourself. Keep things in perspective. Don't forget the excitement that led you to your decision to get married in the

first place. Make sure you spend time together and take care of each other in the process of planning your wedding.

Chapter 2

10 Commandments of Wedding Dress Shopping

The quest for your wedding gown can be one of the most exciting and fun-filled parts of planning for your wedding. Your gown will set the tone for your entire wedding and there are few other times where you will be so lavishly pampered as you are magically transformed into a beautiful bride before your very eyes. But, before you buy your wedding gown, here are ten things that you need to know and do.

1. Get a clear picture of what you want your wedding to look like in your mind.
Close your eyes and envision yourself as a bride. What do you see? Are you going to be walking down an aisle, getting married outside, or uttering your vows by the soft glow of candlelight? Will you be wearing a full ball gown with your hear up and a long flowing veil? Or, are you dressed in a flowing, romantic gown that accentuates your femininity? Write down six adjectives that best describe how you want to look and feel on your wedding day. For example, you may write words such as: traditional, romantic, princess-like, lavish, minimalist, sexy, sophisticated, etc.

2. Try on different silhouettes of gowns to find out what looks best on your figure.
All wedding gowns fall under four basic silhouettes. These are: the ball gown (the most traditional of all categories—it has a full bodice and waistline that leads to a very full skirt), the fit and flare (has a fitted design on the body and flares out around your hip area), the A-line (features vertical seams flowing from the shoulders down to an A-shaped flared skirt) and the sheath (closely follows the line of the body). An experienced bridal consultant can point out the features of how you look in each. You should let her know what you like about each style as well.

3. Select the color and fabric of your gown.

The same dress style can look and feel quite different in another color or fabric. Even though white has traditionally been the color of most gowns, more and more gowns are being designed with color in the details. You may want to consider an off-white, ivory or blush/champagne color as a way to enhance your complexion. Choose a color and fabric that best reflects the mood you are trying to create at your wedding. When choosing the fabric, keep in mind that it will be the basis for the overall look and feel of your gown and will influence cost more than any other single thing. Textured material and overlays such as chiffon, tulle, and organza can also be used to create a special look for you.

4. Determine what features you want on your gown.

These features include the type of neckline, waistline, train, beadwork or lace on the bodice and skirt, and other decorations or embellishments. Once you have determined which silhouette, color, and fabric you like best, determine if the gown will have sleeves, straps, or if you prefer strapless. You will want to try on a variety of gowns to help you find what you like best as you bring "the perfect gown" into closer focus.

5. Accept help from knowledgeable and professional bridal consultants.

A good bridal consultant will ask lots of questions to get more clarity about your special day. They will want to be helpful to you and may have some recommendations for you. An expert consultant has seen gowns on many women in various shapes and sizes and will be able to recommend a dress that will look great on your body. Let an expert's opinion guide you to considering some shapes or styles you might never have imagined wearing. However, your consultant should make you feel comfortable and free to express your own opinion. From the moment you enter the salon, be mindful of the way the salespeople make you feel. Do they treat you with respect? This is your special day and you deserve help that makes you feel comfortable and happy.

6. Be aware of traditions or religious guidelines that may influence how your gown should look.

Different pastors, clergy, or officiants of weddings in various religious, and/or ethnic backgrounds may require that your head, legs, or shoulders be covered. It is best to check with your ceremony officiant to find out if he/she has any guidelines that may need to be considered before you buy your gown. This will prevent embarrassment on the part of you and your guests.

7. Bring along someone whose opinion you trust and respect to help you in your search.
This person could be your mother, sister, bridesmaid, honor attendant, a close friend, or another relative. An extra set of eyes can be helpful, but limit the number of people who come with you. Too many opinions will likely confuse you and lead to a frustrating experience. Such feedback can be invaluable. But, remember it is your wedding! So, you should make the final decision after careful consideration of your choices.

8. Make your decision.
Making your final decision doesn't have to be stressful. You have your mother or friend and your consultant to help you. Trust your own instincts. You have likely been visualizing this day for some time. Ask yourself these three questions of the final dresses that you are seriously considering: 1) Which dress do I feel the prettiest in?; 2) Which dress accentuates my best feature?; and 3) Which dress most fits my personality or style? Try on each gown and go through this process until you have eliminated all of the gowns down to the final one. Once you've found a gown that is everything you've imagined, smile and relax—you've done it!

9. Have your dress altered to match your exact figure.
Once you have your gown, find a professional seamstress, who is an expert at altering wedding gowns, to help you make the final alterations that will help your dress fit perfectly. Many bridal stores will have their own seamstress on site to help you. This process usually involves an initial fitting and one to two more alteration appointments. Following these fitting appointments, your dress will be pressed. We recommend you schedule your pressing the week of your wedding and pick it up a few days before your event.

10. Look for the final touches that will help you complete your gown and make your wedding day special.
Once you've found your gown, look for matching elements such as veils, shoes, and accessories that will make your transformation into a new bride complete. You may want to ask your bridal consultant for suggestions for these final touches.

With these ten tips in mind, your quest for your wedding gown should now be an exciting, fulfilling, and wonderful experience.

CHAPTER 3

THE 5 BIGGEST MYTHS ABOUT WEDDING DRESS SHOPPING DEBUNKED

ABC's 20/20 recently did a special entitled "Wedding Confidential" that offered "20 Ways to Cut Wedding Costs." As a part of the interview, they interviewed Denise and Alan Fields who have written a book entitled *Bridal Bargains*. Many of the statements they made in the interview and that they make in the book are patently false and perpetuate myths about the wedding dress shopping experience. Many of their claims insinuate that the majority of wedding professionals are out to rip off brides and scam them out of money as they prepare for their big day.

We started our wedding business to help brides find the perfect dress for their wedding. We didn't go into business to rip people off or to scam them out of money as 20/20 or Denise and Alan Fields seem to suggest. The reality is that we've helped literally thousands of brides from all across the state to find the perfect dress and we've received glowing reviews from these brides who have loved our gowns and who have been absolutely ecstatic about the experience they've had at our store. I hope you'll take the time to read every word of this chapter that debunks seven of the biggest myths about wedding dress shopping.

Myth #1: You'll save money by buying a dress online.
One of the big myths that many brides fall prey to today (that they most regret) is that of buying a dress online. Some brides claim they have had a good experience buying from an online Chinese company, but the vast majority of brides encounter serious heartbreak and frustration when making this choice. It is so heartbreaking seeing brides come into our store in tears who have lost money and received a shockingly, terrible gown. Much of the advice to buy a wedding dress online that you'll see is seriously

outdated. That advice doesn't include how many of the online sources for fake and counterfeit dresses (which are constructed out of cheap fabrics with glued on appliqués and beading) are being shut down in conjunction with work done by the ABPIA (American Bridal and Prom Industry Association), US Customs, and Homeland Security. Legal injunctions that have been made against forty of the top counterfeit sites are spreading to the other similar web sites as well. Even if a web site promotes testimonials from "happy brides", many brides are finding out now that the dress they just ordered will never arrive because the dress has been destroyed when it enters the country as a contraband item or the money paid has been seized.

So, what does this mean for you if you are considering buying a dress online? This means simply that going forward you will be less and less likely to actually receive a dress that is ordered from one of these counterfeit sites. It also means that you are very likely guaranteed that the money you pay to a counterfeiter will be lost entirely—since payment to any company that is found supporting an illegal trade is shut down. Many of these injunctions are designed to freeze the assets of the companies who engage in this type of trade. If a dress enters the United States as an illegal item, it is considered contraband by US Customs and will be destroyed. This legal battle will continue as time goes on and more and more counterfeiter sites will be shut down. This will cause those brides who make the choice to buy online to lose their money and be shattered by disappointment.

Buying a wedding dress for the most important day of your life shouldn't be left to chance. At our store, we don't want you or any bride to suffer the consequences of having a poorly made copy crafted from cheap fabrics and glued on beading to ruin your day. Type in "Internet Wedding Dress Disasters" into Google and you'll find hundreds of brides who have been absolutely devastated by their choice to buy a dress online. Believe me, you really don't want a dress that will fall apart or have the zipper break on you when you are standing in front of hundreds of guests. At our store, we want you to be thrilled with your dress purchase and help you find a dress that fits within your budget. We have hundreds of exquisite gowns to pick from and invite you to come into the store so you can see for yourself why our gowns are considered by brides in our area to be the very best.

With all that you have to worry about with planning the wedding of your dreams, you really don't need the extra stress and hassle of worrying that your dress may not come in correctly or be perfect for your wedding day. Why take the risk? When you order your gown from a full service bridal salon, you can be assured that we'll take care of all of the details. You'll be glad you did because you won't have to stress about the mess that could have happened with your dress.

Myth #2: Don't go to businesses with "weddings" in the name because they will automatically mark everything up.
The recent special on 20/20 asserted that wedding vendors are out to rip you off and demonstrated this by showing a behind the scenes example where they called a DJ and asked the price to DJ a birthday party and a wedding on the same date. The price was different and the quote for the wedding service was higher than the regular party services. The assertion made by 20/20 was that if you buy from a place that has the name "weddings" in the name, you would be charged more for a service. The reality is that while there may be a small number of crooks in the wedding industry (as there are in any industry who try to gouge with higher prices), these types of services may be quoted different amounts because there is much more time and planning involved in putting together a wedding versus a birthday celebration.

As bridal store owners, we were more than a little shocked by the assertion that a wedding professional would treat a bride differently depending on if she drove up in a Mercedes or a Geo. We treat all of our brides the same. We don't have one price for a bride who drives up in a Mercedes and another price for a bride who drives up in a Geo. We treat every bride with the dignity and respect we expected in our own wedding planning process. The prices of our gowns are determined by four things: the type of fabric it is constructed from, the amount of lining and inner construction, the type and amount of ornamentation and the skill of the seamstresses who construct our gowns. We have dresses in all price points and so if a bride has a certain budget, we'll work very closely with her to help her get the dress she wants and can afford for her wedding. Everyone at our store works very hard to help the brides we serve. We provide exceptional gowns at an incredible value (especially when you consider all of the gifts and bonuses we give brides who buy from us). But, don't just take our word for it. We invite you to go to other bridal stores and then come into ours. You'll find the atmosphere and the experience at our store to be inviting, relaxing, and most important focused on you—what you're looking for and the wedding you're planning so hard to achieve.

Myth #3: You should rent a wedding dress instead of buying one.
Many brides hear this from a variety of sources. The most commonly held belief is that a rental will only cost you hundreds, whereas buying a wedding dress will cost you thousands. While there are a few places that rent dresses, most of them won't tell you the down and dirty details about what it really costs to rent versus buying a wedding dress. If cost is an issue, we have dresses in our store that you can buy for the same price it would cost you to rent a dress and it will be yours to treasure forever. Your daughter can't pull out and look at the gown you've rented, but the look on her face when she imagines her mother in that gown will be a treasured and priceless memory. The reality is that there aren't that many bridal stores that rent dresses. This is because gowns can only last so long being continuously altered, cleaned and pressed between the dozens of brides who may wear it over the course of its lifetime. When you buy a wedding dress, it will be a gown that only *you* will have worn on your wedding day. Some rental companies say that all of the add on options that you could add will make the cost of buying a wedding dress much more. At our store, we don't sell items to brides that they don't need. Depending on the business, wedding dress rentals typically range from $250 to $600. Gowns are often only delivered 1-3 days before the wedding, and usually must be returned the day following your wedding. A damage deposit of $200+ may also be required and if anything happens to the dress you may end up buying it anyway. On top of that, there are only a few styles available, you can only make minimal alterations to the gown, and the gown may have already been worn multiple times. At a full service bridal salon like our store, we stock hundreds of choices of exquisite gowns that you can choose from and wear on your wedding. You could choose to limit your options by renting; but with all of the beautiful gowns out there, we think you'll discover that there is a reason why very few brides actually end up renting a wedding gown. If you are looking to stay within a certain price range, please let either one of us or your bridal consultant at our store know and we'll be

happy to accommodate the price range you are looking for. Then, you can own your dress and enjoy the memories you've had. Beyond that, you will treasure additional memories when you pull out your wedding dress years from now and show it to your daughters who want to see the gown their mother wore on her wedding day.

Myth #4: You should be able to find a beautiful gown for less than $500. Another variation of this myth: Buy an inexpensive dress and build it up with bling and accessories to make it look nicer.
Many brides today come into bridal salons saying they have budgeted two or three hundred dollars on the low end for a wedding dress and maybe up to five hundred dollars on the high end. They are shocked to find the nearly impossible task of finding a well-made dress in this price range.

Most brides who have insisted on finding a dress in the $99 to $300 price range have found quickly that not all dresses are created equal. Those brides who are so set on a low-end price often end up spending more money on alterations than they did on the price of their dress, because it is so inexpensively made.

In fact, most gowns sold for less than $600 that you see heavily advertised and promoted by the big box retailers are made from synthetic fabrics that have minimal construction details. They are actually made this way by the store's request to cut costs. These dresses usually have minimal lining (if any, so you can actually see your underwear through the dress), have minimal boning (if any at all) and are missing other structural supports to help the dress fit properly. These supports are extremely important as both boning and underlining fabrics help to hold the bodice of a dress up and securely in place. They also help provide a smooth fit over the bodice of the dress. If a dress doesn't have boning or good lining, you will see more wrinkles and crinkling of the fabric in a wedding dress. The last thing a bride wants to see in her wedding dress is bulges in the fabric of her dress due minimal boning and lack of inner construction.

One claim made by 20/20 in their recent article accompanying their "Wedding Confidential" special is that brides should "buy a plain wedding dress" and then "add accessories to it like starting with a blank canvas."

While it is true that you can add sashes, belts and other accessories to a dress in order to make it prettier, many stunning wedding gowns already have these embellishments built right into the dress and the cost savings really aren't that significant (if they are at all).

Simply put, there are four reasons why wedding dresses cost what they do. These reasons have to do with fabric, lining and inner construction, ornamentation and the skill of the individual constructing the gown. At our store, we want to help you find the perfect dress at a price that will fit within your overall budget. In fact, we are so confident that we can help you find a dress on your first visit, that we would like to offer you a $100 coupon for you to save off the price of any wedding dress you find in our store over $499. We can't wait to see you in our store and help you find the dress of your dreams.

Myth #5: It's better to order a dress than to purchase an in-stock dress. Some brides believe this myth because they think or feel that the dresses they try on at a bridal store have also been tried on by "hundreds" of other brides. This is very unlikely since most bridal retailers bring in brand new gowns to their stores several times each year and they are constantly refreshing their inventory to showcase the latest trends and fashions that brides in their respective areas are looking for. Since this is the case, the dress you try on has likely only been tried on by a handful of brides who all did so under the careful direction and supervision of their bridal consultant (so as to preserve the delicate detail, beadwork and fabric of each gown which is sold to and worn by a bride). This is another reason why it is such a good idea to be decisive when you find the perfect dress. We've seen brides come back extremely frustrated and disappointed because the dress they loved was purchased by another more decisive bride literally hours after they left the store. Don't let that happen to you. Another reason why it is a good idea to buy your dress when you find it is because there typically are extra shipping, handling, and processing fees to special order in a wedding gown. Most bridal retailers get special incentives and pricing on gowns when they purchase in bulk and those same savings aren't available to them if they are only purchasing one gown just for you. You can avoid this extra cost by simply purchasing the gown you found on your first visit.

If you have your heart set on special ordering a gown that will be made for you, we will be happy to assist you in making that happen.

It can be easy to get overwhelmed when you start looking at pictures of wedding gowns and start shopping for a dress. There seem to be literally thousands of styles to choose from. The reality is that all wedding gowns fall into one of four basic silhouettes or cuts as follows:

1. The **ball gown** is the most traditional of the categories and has a fitted bodice and waistline that leads to a very full skirt.
2. The **fit and flare** is fitted to the body and flares out around your hip area. Versions of this include mermaid and trumpet.
3. The **A-line cut** features vertical seams flowing from the shoulders down to an A-shaped flared skirt.
4. The **sheath** closely follows the line of the body.

That's it. Just four silhouettes or styles. When you start shopping, try on one of each silhouette or style. Then, you'll be able to see how you look in each one and find out which one accentuates your best features and makes you feel absolutely beautiful and stunning (as your wedding dress should).

We hope this chapter where we've debunked the top five wedding dress shopping myths has been helpful to you. We want to give you the truth about what is involved in buying a wedding dress. There is so much misinformation out there that can be confusing and scary. We invite you to find out what it means to buy a dress from our store by looking at the pictures, videos and written testimonials of the hundreds of brides who have shared their pictures and experience with us on our web site and social media. When you read their thoughtful comments, you'll know that we are here to serve you and help say yes to a dress that you will love and treasure forever. As a way for you to get to know us and see our commitment to you and your wedding, we have some coupons that you can use as part of our First Visit Advantage Program when you arrive at our store. We know you'll love what you'll see and experience at our store and can't wait to meet you soon.

CHAPTER 4

THE BIGGEST MYTHS WE'VE HEARD FROM BRIDES ABOUT THEIR SHOPPING EXPERIENCE

As a recently engaged bride, you have likely been exposed to a lot of information that will help you plan the perfect wedding. There are many myths and superstitions surrounding weddings which have been passed down from generation to generation and some false things that have been perpetuated by the media (as we discussed in the last chapter). Many of the things you hear today simply aren't true or are just downright hilarious. In fact, many wedding traditions followed today are the result of superstitions created by myth and folklore (particularly surrounding avoiding bad luck and evil spirits) and the original meaning has been lost or forgotten over the years.

So, how do you sort through the voluminous amounts of myth and folklore? How do you pick what will define your wedding as one you will always remember and one that all of your friends and relatives will talk about for years to come? Everyone has an opinion, but how will you know what is just right for you?

Over the years, we've heard many different myths that brides have believed and how they have been relieved to find out that they weren't true—or that they didn't need to worry about them. From all of the things we've personally heard over the years from brides we've worked with or from the bridal consultants in our store, we've put together a list of the top ten most shocking and outrageous wedding dress myths. This list will help you sort through the misinformation and find out what will help you plan your wedding without stress, confusion or worry.

Many myths you'll hear conflict with one another and have different meanings. Many have supposedly been used to foretell good and bad luck. Even though most myths brides hear aren't true, it doesn't stop them from going all out to make sure they haven't missed anything and to ensure that their wedding will be great. Our goal in sharing these top ten dress myths is to help you know what they are and why they aren't true. That way, you can say yes to your dress with confidence and excitement. The top ten myths and our thoughts about them are:

Wedding Dress Myth #1: A wedding dress should be white. You shouldn't wear a white wedding gown if you're not a virgin or if it is your second or third marriage.
The most popular color of wedding dresses today is ivory. The color white was traditionally chosen to imitate the color of Queen Victoria's dress when she wed Albert in 1840. While, many have embraced that tradition, the reality is that prior to that time, the majority of wedding gowns were either silver or red. Today, brides can choose whatever color they wish, whether they are virgins or not, and whether it is their first marriage, second or third. The only thing that matters regarding the color of your wedding gown is that it is a color that *you want* to wear. Quite simply, it is your choice.

One funny poem written in the 1800s that describes a bride's fate depending on the color of dress she got married in reveals the silliness of traditions regarding color.

"Married in White, you have chosen right
Married in Grey, you will go far away,
Married in Black, you will wish yourself back,
Married in Red, you will wish yourself dead,
Married in Green, ashamed to be seen,
Married in Blue, you will always be true,
Married in Pearl, you will live in a whirl,
Married in Yellow, ashamed of your fellow,
Married in Brown, you will live in the town,

Married in Pink, your spirit will sink."

Again, it is your wedding and you can choose whatever color dress you would like to wear so that you'll feel beautiful and comfortable. That is what matters most of all.

Wedding Dress Myth #2: I've got lots of time, as I'm not getting married for six months to a year.
Following your engagement, it is easy to get caught in the trap that you've got lots of time as you plan your wedding. However, as you've probably discovered, time passes quickly and it takes time to construct and complete the intricate details that a wedding gown requires. *Brides* magazine recommends that you get your dress at least a year before you get married. There is so much to do as you plan your wedding and your dress will be the centerpiece of everything you do. By getting that decision out of the way, you'll be able to focus on all of the other details that will go into planning your perfect wedding experience.

Wedding Dress Myth #3: In order to find the perfect dress, you have to look endlessly on web sites and try on lots of gowns at every store in town.
It is easy to get overwhelmed when you start looking at pictures of wedding gowns. There seem to be literally thousands of styles to choose from. The reality is that all wedding gowns fall into one of four basic silhouettes or cuts. As a review, these are:
- The **ball gown** is the most traditional of the categories and has a fitted bodice and waistline that leads to a very full skirt).
- The **fit and flare** is fitted to the body and flares out around your hip area. Versions of this include mermaid and trumpet.
- The **A-line cut** features vertical seams flowing from the shoulders down to an A-shaped flared skirt.
- The **sheath** closely follows the line of the body.

There truly are just four silhouettes or styles. When you start shopping, we recommend you try on one of each silhouette or style. That way, you'll be able to see how you look in each one and find out which one accentuates your best features and makes you feel absolutely beautiful and stunning (as your wedding dress should).

Wedding Dress Myth #4: You shouldn't start shopping until you are the size you want to be on your wedding day.
Another variation of this myth is that a wedding dress must fit you perfectly before you can buy it. Planning a wedding can be a very stressful experience and stress is a well-known and proven cause of weight fluctuation. In our experience, at least 98% of all of the dresses that brides buy at our store require some type of alterations. If you are planning to lose weight, it is easy and inexpensive to adjust the gown you've chosen to fit you closer to your wedding day. The problem with waiting is that you limit your choices (since gowns require time to order). Also, it's critical to realize that a gown you love may be sold to another decisive bride. The majority of brides buy their dresses nine to eighteen months prior to their weddings with this in mind. They know they should get their alterations done closer to the date of the wedding. They plan ahead and ensure that they'll get the dress they love most and then alter it to fit perfectly right before the wedding. If you wait, you may have to scramble to find the dress you want and pay extra in alterations and rush fees that could have been avoided with planning. A good rule of thumb is to buy the dress that best fits you now. You can always alter it down if you lose weight. If you don't, then you don't have to stress out. Remember, your gown can be altered to fit you perfectly and your fiancé loves you just as you are. Don't forget that you'll relieve a lot of the stress of planning your wedding once you have your dress (since you'll be able to focus on the many other decisions that go into planning your wedding). Plus, a knowledgeable and competent seamstress can sculpt the dress you've chosen to fit you like a glove.

Wedding Dress Myth #5: You shouldn't buy the first dress you try on at the first store you've visited.
This common belief is really an extension of Myth #3—that you have to look and look until you find the perfect dress. While it is a good idea to look to ensure that you make the best choice (it is your wedding after all), it is a myth to believe that you can't buy a dress you love at the first store you've visited. After all, you have great taste and are going to pick beautiful dresses from any store that you go to. A large percentage of brides end up buying the first dress they try on for this reason. Their eye is drawn to a dress they *really* love and they end up getting that first dress they tried on. Brides who are indecisive usually come back and end up buying that dress. Unfortunately, this is after they've spent time and money on gasoline by driving all over. That is, money that they could have easily saved by trusting their instincts and getting the dress they loved when they first tried it on. At Something New Boutique, we even have a special incentive for decisive brides who buy on their first visit. We are able to offer this special savings since we have the price of two visits built into every dress. When brides choose to buy the dress they love most on their first visit, we pass those savings along to them. Trust your instincts. You may not find your dress at the first store you go to; but if you do, don't hesitate to begin enjoying the euphoric feeling you'll have knowing you have already taken care *that* part of your wedding!

Wedding Dress Myth #6: If it is meant to be, it won't be sold before I come back.
It is easy to get caught up in the notion of fate and that things happen for a reason. The opposite is also true. Sometimes things happen for no reason at all and for reasons that can't be explained. When you find your dress, it is best to decide to get it then— instead of letting another bride and her mother decide for you. At Something New Boutique, we dress thousands of brides each year. We are busy and on multiple occasions we've seen brides who have trusted fate wake up to the realization that the dress they loved most had been sold. They cried, pleaded and begged for us

to help them get another dress in, but many times it just isn't possible. The question you have to ask yourself is this: If you've found your dress, why would you let another bride and her mother tell you what you will or won't be wearing your wedding day? Isn't that a decision you'd rather make? Believe me, you don't want to return to a store you've visited hoping your dress is still there and then leave crushed that it has already been sold. Unfortunately, we've seen that happen on too many occasions and we don't want to see it happen to you. When you find your dress, take control. Don't let the dress of your dreams slip through your fingers and let someone else make the decision for you. You've done the hard work and found your dress. Go ahead and get the dress you love and you'll be absolutely ecstatic leaving the store that no one can take the dress you've found away from you. On top of that, you'll save money by buying your dress on your first visit. You can use that savings for something else that you're planning for your wedding. Don't let the myth of fate determine the consequences of your decisions for you. You decided to marry your best friend and you should also decide to get the dress you love (not let someone else make that decision for you).

Wedding Dress Myth #7: It's cheaper if you or someone you know makes your wedding dress.

There is an old myth that says, "The bride should not make her own wedding dress; for each stitch up of the wedding garb the bride sews herself she'll shed one tear during her marriage." This old saying obviously has no scientific basis. While it is usually cheaper to do things yourself, such is not the case today with wedding gowns. All wedding gowns are sewn by hand and are done so by artisans and professionals who have years of experience in constructing gowns day in and day out. There are many intricate details that go into making a wedding gown. On some of the dresses in our store, there are over 10,000 individual beads that are sewn onto each individual dress, all by hand. It takes 38 days for one highly skilled seamstress just to sew on all of the beadwork, not to mention all of the other aspects of delicately placing each piece of boning and fabric to make a work of art. If you are blessed to have a talented seamstress in your family, you are a lucky bride indeed. However, even talented seamstresses recognize that wedding gowns that are produced at the best factories have a level of detail and attention that even they can't match or re-create. At Something New Boutique, we are able to offer gowns at prices much lower than what a close family member can make a gown for (especially if you factor in all of the time it takes to create the gown and do all of the fittings). Do yourself a favor and let that special someone in your life help you do the alterations; and, trust the wedding artisans who construct our gowns to take care of all of the details to make your stunning dress. Regardless of this advice, many brides still choose to have someone else make their dress only to discover weeks before the wedding that it didn't turn out right or fit correctly. In the end, they've had to scramble to get a different dress (causing tremendous stress and anxiety). Don't let this happen to you.

Wedding Dress Myth #8: Buying a dress online will save you money.
This is a common perception of many brides who mistakenly believe the price they see online guarantees they'll get service on their gown purchase. What happens when you buy a dress online versus buying it at a full service bridal salon is dramatically different. We recently had a bride named Jessica who experienced this dramatic difference first hand. She came into our store in tears because the dress she received looked completely different than the picture she saw online. The lace was different, the seams were loose and crooked, there was no boning or support, and the dress bulged in certain areas. The company she purchased the dress from wouldn't refund her money and she was left to either fix what she had (which didn't give her a lot of options) or buy a new dress. She ended up buying a new dress at our store and wished she had done that in the first place. When you buy a dress from Something New Boutique, you'll notice that:
- You will get connected with the best seamstress so your dress will be perfectly altered to your figure and pressed so

that it is wrinkle-free and looks absolutely stunning on your wedding day. An online purchase will arrive wrinkled in a box and you'll have to pay more to have it pressed.

- Any beads that may have come loose during shipping or the alterations process will be tightened at no charge. An online purchase leaves you on your own. You'll have to pay to fix any beads that are loose or that have popped off.

- You can be assured that there won't be any spots or stains on your dress when you pick it up. Every dress we sell goes through our comprehensive 5-point premium care treatment process. When you purchase a gown online, you really don't know what you'll get. A dress purchased at our store ensures you'll get exactly what you thought and more.

- Your dress will be perfectly sculpted to your figure and you'll know that it will come in the right size. Buying a dress online is a gamble because you don't know if the size chart you saw online will really match the dress you're buying. At our store, what you see and experience will change your belief about buying anything online ever again, forever.

- Lastly, your dress will look like the sample you ordered it from and you won't have to worry about any of the details.

With all that you have to worry about with planning the wedding of your dreams, you really don't need the extra stress and hassle of worrying that your dress may not come in correctly or be perfect for your wedding day. Why take the risk? When you order your gown from Something New Boutique, you can be assured that we'll take care of all of the details. You'll be glad you did. You won't have to stress about the mess that could have happened with your dress.

Wedding Dress Myth #9: If you don't cry, it's not "the" dress. People feel emotions differently in varying situations. Not everyone cries when they see a touching movie or hear a tragic or moving story. The way you'll feel when you find "the dress" will likely be very different from how a well-meaning friend or family member may have felt when they found their wedding gown. Just because they may have cried when they found their dress, doesn't mean that you will as well. Less than 30 percent of the thousands of brides we've helped to find their dress have cried when they made their decision. Instead of crying, these brides typically feel very excited and love to move around in their gown. They become possessive of the gown they're in and visualize themselves getting married on their wedding day. Another part of this myth is that if everyone in my wedding party doesn't like your dress, you shouldn't get it.

Wedding Dress Myth #10: It is better to order a dress than to purchase an in-stock dress.
Some brides believe this myth because they think or feel that the dresses they try on at a bridal store have also been tried on by "hundreds" of other brides. As mentioned before, this is very unlikely since most bridal retailers bring in brand new gowns to their stores several times each year and they are constantly refreshing their inventory to showcase the latest trends and fashions that brides in their respective areas are looking for. Since this is the case, the dress you try on has likely only been tried on by a handful of brides who all did so under the careful direction and supervision of their bridal consultant (so as to preserve the delicate detail, beadwork and fabric of each gown which is sold to and worn by a bride).

This is another reason why it is such a good idea to be decisive when you find the perfect dress. We've seen brides come back extremely frustrated and disappointed because the dress they loved was purchased by another more decisive bride literally hours after they left the store. Don't let that happen to you. Another reason why it is a good idea to buy your dress when you find it out of stock is because there is an extra shipping, handling, and processing fee to order in a gown this way. Most bridal retailers get special incentives and pricing on gowns when they purchase in bulk and those same savings aren't available to them if they are only purchasing one gown just for you. You can avoid this extra cost by simply purchasing the gown you found on your first visit. If you have you heart set on special ordering a gown that will be made for you, we will be happy to assist you in making this happen.

We hope this chapter on the biggest regrets we've heard about the shopping experience from brides has been helpful to you. You'll receive several coupons that you can use on your dress and other items at your first visit. Please call us to schedule your appointment now or visit our web site www.somethingnewboutique.com and we'll help you say yes to a dress that you will love and treasure forever. We look forward to meeting you at Something New Boutique soon.

CHAPTER 5

THE MYTH OF THE $99-$399 WEDDING DRESS:
WHY DRESSES COST WHAT THEY DO AND BUDGETING FOR YOUR WEDDING DRESS

Following engagement, many brides discover that things are much more expensive than they thought they would be, particularly when it comes to a wedding dress. Many brides today come into bridal salons saying they have budgeted two or three hundred dollars on the low end for a wedding dress and maybe up to five hundred dollars on the high end. They are shocked to find the nearly impossible task of finding a well-made dress in this price range.

Most brides who have insisted on finding a dress in the $99 to $300 price range have found quickly that all dresses are not created equal. Those brides who are so set on a low-end price often end up spending more money on alterations than they did on the price of their dress because it is so inexpensively made.

As we shared before, most gowns that are sold for less than $600 that you see heavily advertised and promoted by the big box retailers are made from synthetic fabrics that have minimal construction details and are made this way by the store's request to their manufacturer to cut costs.

If you have been feeling stressed by the cost of your wedding and in particular a number you've budgeted for your wedding dress, this chapter we've written is just for you. We'd hate for you to make a mistake with such an important purchase that will be one of the focal points of your big day (especially since everyone will see you in it and will comment on how you look).

In this chapter, we'll explore how myths like the $99 to $300 wedding dress have appeared and why wedding dresses cost what they do. We'll also share with you several insights into how wedding gowns are constructed so you can be sure you are getting the best value for your money. Most importantly, we have a coupon that we'll share with you as a thank you for reading this book that you'll be able to save off the purchase price of your wedding dress when you buy it on your first visit to our store.

The initial sticker shock of wedding dresses may have come as a surprise to you. Why does a dress you'll wear one day of your life seem to cost so much?

As, has already been mentioned, there are four reasons and they all encompass various aspects of how the dress is made. Let's go into a little bit more detail for each reason.

Fabric
The first reason is fabric. This is what makes up the majority of the dress. Within each type of fabric, there are also many different grades or quality of fabric. Dresses can be made of silk, various types and varying grades of satin, chiffon, and organza. Many dresses today are also draped with exquisite lace.

Most moderately priced wedding gowns ($600 to $2000) are constructed from much higher quality fabrics and ornamentation and use higher-grade fabrics that drape more elegantly and show off their versatility in design. The ornamentation and beading that is sewn onto these dresses is also of a much higher quality. There are varying degrees of inner construction and most all dresses in this price range are fully underlined for stability and to give your finished dress a smoother appearance as it drapes across your figure. These dresses usually have some crinoline built into the skirt to provide additional support to that part of the dress.

As was mentioned, a very important part of the fabric that makes up a wedding dress is its lining. Lower priced gowns usually don't have any lining at all. As the price of wedding dresses increases, you'll find variations in the transparency and opulence of the fabrics that are used. In fact, some of the fabrics used for the inner lining on more expensive or couture dresses could be used as the outer fabric of many beautiful gowns. The difference in the thickness, thread count, and overall quality of the lining makes a huge difference in how well the dress flows, and most importantly, how it fits. Gowns that have very inexpensive lining often cause the outer part of your dress to make creases in the dress that won't flatter your figure.

Many dress manufacturers and big box retailers are able to offer dresses for seemingly low prices by cutting corners with less expensive dress linings or by using no lining at all underneath a dress.

Fit and Inner Construction
Probably the biggest thing you'll notice when looking at the inside of a wedding dress (that indicates high quality and construction) is how the inner bodice of a wedding dress is made. The most expensive and highest quality gowns often have a built in bustier with boning that will flatter the figure of anyone in the dress. Some of these gowns are quite elaborate and exquisite. When you come in for your appointment, please ask to see the inner construction of these gowns. You'll be amazed by the attention to detail and the way the dress will fit on you. In fact, many brides tell us that this is what draws them to buy one dress over another – how it fits and how they feel in it (which is all influenced by the inner construction of a gown).

Workmanship
There are literally hundreds of hours of work in the construction of every single wedding gown we sell at our store. It is easy for some brides to want to buy a wedding gown for a price of $99 or

$299 without having any consideration for the amount of time and the sheer talent that goes into constructing, and hand-stitching every bead and bit of appliqué onto a dress. Most of the dresses in our store sell between $700 and $2000. When you look closely at what goes into the construction of each gown, you would be absolutely amazed and floored by how inexpensively you can wear such a beautiful work of art on your wedding day. As an example, it takes one highly skilled seamstress twenty-three eight-hour days to sew on more than 10,000 beads on one of the dresses in our store.

To appreciate the level of skill and workmanship this requires, time yourself sewing fifty beads (in three different colors) onto a piece of fabric in just a straight line, much less an intricate and beautiful pattern. How long would it take you to sew on these fifty beads? You can't make a mistake and put two of the same colored beads together and the beads must be sewn on by hand, one-by-one. Once you have spent a few minutes threading a needle, sticking yourself with the needle, having the needle get unthreaded again, etc. you really begin to appreciate the talent and skill the dressmakers have who construct each and every one of the beautiful gowns you see in our store by hand.

The skilled professionals who sew each and every dress in our store have spent years mastering their craft and take tremendous pride in their work. Shopping for a dress with only a dollar number in mind, discounts the tremendous efforts that are put forward by skilled professionals who have dedicated themselves to true mastery.

Most inexpensive wedding gowns that are priced under $500 are often made by less skilled artisans who are just beginning the process of learning how to make wedding gowns.

Ornamentation
Another important aspect of what makes up the overall cost of a wedding dress is its ornamentation. In fact, much of a gown's

personality is made up in the type and amount of ornamentation it has. Dresses are often adorned with seed pearls, Swarovski crystals, and exquisite appliqués with corresponding beading. A big part of the cost of a wedding dress (especially the most expensive ones) is the quality of the little details that make up your dress.

One of the biggest aspects of ornamentation is the train of a wedding gown. Anciently, the length of the train was an indication of the amount of wealth the bride's family possessed. The longer the train, the wealthier you were. It was a status symbol and a way to show off your wealth to those who were invited to the wedding. Today, the type and length of train is most likely an indication of the formality or informality of the wedding. Longer trains tend to be more formal and less formal gowns typically have smaller court or sweep trains.

Since there are many types of ornamentation, we recommend that you settle on a silhouette or cut before you consider all of the different types of ornamentation. The fit is really one of the most important features you should consider. Then, you can find a dress in that cut with the ornamentation that will best set the tone you want to create at your wedding.

That's it. Those are the four biggest things that make up the price of a dress. Now, when you go to a bridal store, you'll know why dresses cost what they do. You'll also understand the myth of the $99 wedding gown. This myth has been primarily promoted by big box retailers who use this low, low price as a tantalizing hook to get you into their stores. In reality, there are usually very few if any wedding dresses in that price range that are also in your size. And more importantly, you won't likely like the cheap dress for a lack of one of the reasons mentioned above.

How much you end up spending on your dress is completely up to you. We hope that this chapter has been helpful to you in determining why a dress costs what it does so you can be more realistic in your budget assessment for your dress. Nothing is more frustrating for a bride who drives to every bridal shop and spends hundreds of dollars in time, money, and gas looking for the perfect $100 dress that doesn't exist.

Some brides will be super-focused on finding a dress in this price range and then be devastated later to find that she spent more on alterations to fix the dress to fit her figure. She could have had the dress she really wanted if she would have budgeted a little more and got what she really wanted that fit her right in the first place. There is no reason for you to make this same mistake.

Now you know that there is a reason why wedding dresses cost what they do. At Something New Boutique, we want to help you find the perfect dress at a price that will fit within your overall budget. We invite you to go to www.somethingnewboutique.com or call us to schedule an appointment to try on dresses. We can't wait to see you in our store and help you find the dress of your dreams.

SECTION 2:
THE DRESS

Chapter 6

7 Rules for Dress Shopping that Will Make It Easier for You to Say Yes to Your Dress

Now that you're engaged, you may feel a little overwhelmed with everything there is to do as you plan for your wedding. In past chapters, we've discussed several of the things you need to know before you buy a wedding dress as well as some common myths about dresses—including what dresses cost. Now, as you begin the search for *your* dress, we've put together the seven most important rules you need to follow when you go shopping for your dress. Some of them we have talked about before, but if you see something repeated it is because we don't want you to forget and because we've seen heartbreak because one of these rules was violated. We don't want that to happen to you. Here are the seven rules:

1. **Have a realistic price range in mind when shopping for your dress.**
There are four things that go into the price of every wedding dress you'll try on from the type of fabric, the extent of the lining & inner construction, the type of ornamentation, and the skill of the seamstress who actually makes your dress. Many brides who go shopping for a wedding dress have a number in mind when they go shopping. Experts recommend that this number can be from 15 to 20% of the total amount of your wedding budget. We have a wide range of price ranges at our store. We have been told time and time again by brides all across the state that we have the best selection they've ever seen in every price range imaginable. In the last chapter, we discussed why it is a myth to pay a little and get a lot for a wedding gown. While there are dresses in a variety of

price ranges, most manufacturers have cut corners in one of the four areas we mentioned above to offer a dress for a low price that may not be a good fit for your wedding. We would encourage you to read this chapter carefully so you can go into the experience of dress shopping with your eyes wide open and make an informed decision about what you'll be wearing when you publicly declare your love and union to the world.

2. **Limit who you bring shopping with you.**

When you announce your engagement, you'll have lots of friends who will want to go shopping with you. No matter how much they beg and plead you don't have to bring them with you. In fact, you may find that bringing multiple people with you only means that you are going to hear multiple opinions. Usually these opinions are spoken based on what they would wear, not necessarily what you want to wear on your wedding date. As a result, many brides who have brought more than three people with them have told us that it was one of the biggest mistakes they made in preparation for their wedding. One recent bride told us that she nearly left the store crying because her well-meaning friends overwhelmed her with contradictory comments and one of her friends really hurt her feelings because of what she said about the dress she actually picked to wear on her wedding day. You don't want this kind of drama when you go shopping, so just bring your mother and one or two of your closest friends or family members whose opinion you trust. If you bring more, you are asking for a smorgasbord of opinions, none of which will matter more than your own.

3. **Plan for your appointment to take from about an hour to no more than ninety minutes.**

In this time you'll be able to try on the four silhouettes of wedding gowns. We'll show those to you when you arrive along with the five main types of fabric from which the majority of wedding gowns are made. Within an hour of entering the store, you should have a very clear idea of what you're looking for and, very likely you will have narrowed down your choice to a couple of favorites.

Your bridal consultant can give you three helpful questions and tips that will help you decide, so you can say "yes" to your dress.

4. **Be sure to eat at least an hour before you arrive at your appointment.**

That way, you can focus on the experience of finding the perfect dress instead of thinking about eating or feeling hungry. On an occasion as important as your wedding, you don't want to feel light headed when you're carefully considering which dress you'll be wearing when you and your fiancé are married.

5. **Bringing children with you to your appointment will be a decision everyone in your party will regret.**

A bridal salon is not a very exciting place for a young child and they will lose interest very quickly in what you are doing and will want to explore. As a result, you and other members of your party will likely be distracted from focusing on you and helping you find your dress. Have someone else watch the little ones and you'll be much happier with the outcome.

6. **Tell your consultant what you are thinking and feeling.**

Your bridal consultant is there to help you find your dress. It doesn't hurt her feelings or the feelings of a dress if you don't like something you try on. Please be open and honest with her about what you like and what you don't like. When you are open with her, she can offer suggestions and recommendations that can help you have a more rewarding experience and find the dress much quicker.

7. **Saying "yes" to your dress isn't harder than it was to say "yes" to your fiancé's proposal for marriage.**

Every member of our professional staff is here to help you find the dress you love most. Once you find it, you won't necessarily be overcome by emotion. Remember, everyone feels emotions in different ways, depending on the situation. When you you're your dress, don't over think it. Simply enjoy the moment instead of trying to force any emotion you thought you might feel when you find your dress.

Now, that you've learned the 7 Rules of Dress Shopping, here are 7 specific things about Something New Boutique that you won't find anywhere else.

1. At our store, you'll enjoy an incredible selection of gowns you won't find anywhere else in the state. We are involved in every aspect of the selection of all of the exquisite gowns you'll find at Something New Boutique. Great care goes into ensuring that we have dresses that are not only unique, but truly on the cutting edge of fashion.

2. Our huge selection of gowns in sizes 0-28 will allow you to be able to try on your gown in your size.

3. Every gown purchased at our store goes through our proprietary 5-Point Premium Care Treatment process. Whether you purchase your gown from our in-stock selection or special order your gown, you are assured of an absolutely stunning wedding gown that will be exquisitely prepared for your wedding day.

4. Something New Boutique is one of the most highly recommended locally owned bridal salons in the entire state of Colorado. We have personally assisted thousands of brides over the years!

5. When you arrive at our boutique, you'll find several great savings options that you'll receive when you purchase your dress with our First Visit Advantage Program. This will allow you to save up to $300 on your wedding dress and accessories if you buy your dress on your first visit. We also have coupons and rewards for your bridesmaids and other members of your wedding party that you can't get anywhere else. Finally, we have a FREE gift waiting for you that you have to see to believe! (that is ONLY available to our brides who schedule an appointment)

6. Our brides can get back every penny of the money they've

spent on their wedding gown (minus the sales tax) up to one year from the purchase date with our easy referral program.

7.   Be sure to ask about a coupon you can get on your first visit to save up to $300 on your wedding dress and accessories simply by scheduling an appointment at **(719) 282-6500 or www.somethingnewboutique.com**. We can't wait to have you in our store and help you prepare for one of the most meaningful and special days of your life!

7 Reasons Why Shopping at Something New Boutique is Better than Visiting 5-6 Other Bridal Stores

Many brides who begin the process of looking for a wedding gown feel that they must visit every store in town to ensure that they've seen every dress and had a chance to explore every option before buying their wedding dress. This chapter is designed to help you see why shopping at Something New Boutique (SNB) is the same as visiting five or six other bridal stores. In addition, we'll share with you four other BIG benefits that you'll get by buying your dress at our store that you won't get anywhere else.

First of all, at SNB, we offer the largest and finest selection of hand-crafted designer wedding gowns in this entire region. Each year, we travel around the world and carefully hand-select the finest fabrics and materials that make up each gown at our store.

Our one-of-a-kind gowns, like our Divina bridal line, have earned rave reviews from the brides who have worn them on their wedding day. When you come to SNB, not only will you find unique and exclusive gowns that you won't find anywhere else, but you'll meet our professional wedding consultants who are dedicated to help you find the perfect gown for your unforgettable day.

Second, from the moment you walk into our doors to the moment you get married, you'll find helpful consultants who will be with you every step of the way to help you find the dress you love without any high pressure that you may have experienced at other bridal shops. Brides tell us that they feel cared for and treated as part of our family at our store. But, don't just take our word for it. We invite you to read the online comments and in-store notes of brides from all over Colorado and surrounding states who have purchased their gown from SNB. You'll see first hand how they felt upon purchasing a dress from SNB and the difference it made in their wedding planning experience.

Third, there is a difference in how you will be treated when you come to SNB. From the moment you enter our beautiful boutique, you'll feel the difference of working with one of our warm, helpful consultants. Not only will you find a new approach to bridal shopping, you'll find that your interaction with one of our honest, caring, and experienced bridal consultants is unlike any other salon you have ever visited.

Fourth, when you come to our store, you'll discover what it's like to work with one of America's Best Bridal Retailers. At SNB, we are grateful to have years of outstanding awards from The Knot, Wedding Wire, designer bridal lines, local media in Colorado, and more.

Fifth, as one of the largest bridal stores in the state, coming to SNB is genuinely equivalent to going to five or six other bridal salons who don't have near the selection or styles that we do. We have a generous selection of each of the four cuts of gowns in your size so you are *bound* to find the perfect dress on your first visit.

Sixth, if you are decisive and find your dress on your first visit, we will reward you our first visit advantage program. Please call our store to get all of the details on how this will benefit you. That's a BIG deal and one we offer because we have the price of two visits built into the price of every dress. When you are decisive, we can pass that savings along to you and you can use that money for many of the other things you will need for your big day—or you can just spend it on yourself.

Seventh, at SNB, we pull out all of the stops to make your shopping experience at our boutique one you'll always treasure and never forget. You'll be amazed at the attention to detail we will provide for you and all of the personal touches that will make shopping for your wedding gown an amazing moment. We are not only the home of Colorado's Best Wedding Dresses; but, more importantly, the bridal boutique, "Where the girl comes before the dress". You'll receive recommendations from one of our highly trained bridal consultant and have the opportunity to try on each of the four silhouettes of wedding dresses as you narrow down your choices to the perfect dress!

Finally, when you arrive, we'll give you a short tutorial on the most important things you need to know before you buy your wedding dress. Within the first few minutes of experiencing this educational tutorial, you'll know you've arrived at the best store to find your wedding dress and the anticipation of finding your dress will skyrocket as your bridal consultant leads you into your dressing room for an amazing experience. You'll be able to try on your gown in your size, take it home with you when you find it and leave with a sense of satisfaction and relief that this part of your wedding planning is completed.

We can't wait to meet you and help you find your wedding dress. You can schedule an appointment by calling us at **(719) 282-6500** or by visiting us on our web site at: www.somethingnewboutique.com.

CHAPTER 8

THE BIG APPOINTMENT: WHO AND WHAT YOU SHOULD BRING WITH YOU AS YOU SHOP FOR YOUR DRESS

Congratulations on your recent engagement and hopefully at this point, you've actually scheduled an appointment at Something New Boutique (SNB). The rest of this chapter will be based on that assumption, so if you haven't scheduled your appointment yet, please do so now. We are so excited to assist you in the search for your wedding gown and can't wait to meet you and work closely with you as you search for the dress you'll wear on your big day!

Now, that you've scheduled your appointment, here are a few tips and suggestions for you that will help make your shopping experience at SNB even more rewarding and exciting! We look forward to working with you. One thing is for certain: You *will* have fun while finding the perfect fit bridal gown at SNB!

TIP #1: If your appointment is scheduled on the weekend, please note that we only have room for you and up to two additional guests per bride. In fact, when shopping for your wedding gown, all the bridal magazine experts advise NOT to bring too many people. Your mom and one other trusted individual seem to be the perfect mix. While everyone will want to come with you on your appointment we ask that you restrict your number of guests. Our rooms only have limited seating options for onlookers. We encourage you to bring those with you whose opinions *you* trust the most. Sometimes too many opinions will confuse you and possibly hurt your feelings. Again, it has been our experience that people often want you to wear what *they* want, not what *you* want. The ultimate decision is yours alone. There will be a time and place for all of the others who want to see the gown you've chosen. Don't worry—after you've bought your dream bridal gown, we can make another appointment for your bridesmaids to choose their gowns!

One final reminder: **It is strongly recommended not to bring children or babies to a bridal store.** If you or the friends who shop with you have children, arrange for a sitter. Your wedding gown choice is one of the most important decisions you will make for your wedding and you don't want to be worrying about where they may have run off to or worry about them getting hurt by loose pins or other hazards. It is so important that you can focus and concentrate on your decision without distractions because you'll be looking of pictures of yourself in the gown you'll chose for the rest of your married life.

TIP #2: Be prepared! Our gowns sell quickly and we want you to get the gown you love most! So, be prepared to purchase your gown the same day you visit. If you wait, the gown you love may not be available on a subsequent visit. To help you better prepare for your appointment, please review the information on "what to expect" that our boutique will send you before your appointment.

Also, you should be prepared by how you dress and what you wear that day. Here are a couple of really important reminders:

- Before you go dress shopping, make sure you're freshly bathed and scrubbed, and wear undies (no thongs, please!)
- Remember to wear nude undergarments. Seamless and nude-colored undergarments will lie flat and undetectable under your dress and will prevent visible panty lines under figure-hugging gowns.
- Avoid hair spray and perfume, and don't apply hand or body lotion, unless it will have at least an hour to be absorbed. It's even more important to avoid tanning solutions. They can ruin a gown if the color smears.

- Leave food and drink outside the store.

You'll probably notice that our bridal consultants will wait on you more closely than you're used to when shopping for other clothing. Don't worry. It's their job to help you find the dress of your dreams and it's also their responsibility to be good stewards of the store's expensive, delicate wedding gowns that brides will wear on their wedding day. So don't feel crowded if your bridal consultant comes right into the dressing room to assist you. Enjoy the attention!

TIP #3: Be decisive and save money! We have the cost of two visits factored into the price of each of each of our wedding gowns. As a reminder, if you can be decisive on your first visit, we will pass those savings on to you. If you wait to get your dress on a subsequent visit, unfortunately you won't be able to get those same savings. In today's economy, we are offering this special incentive to decisive brides who are ready to start enjoying the experience they'll have at our store right away.

We don't want you to miss out on these savings, so get ready for some fun as come in for your appointment and we will work closely with you to help you find the dress of your dreams on your first visit!

As we mentioned previously, we have a free gift waiting for you at our store just for visiting. All you have to do to claim it is bring your copy of this book with you to your appointment.

We are looking forward to meeting you and getting to know exactly what you are looking for as you plan your wedding day. Don't forget – You can request your coupon by emailing us at: info@somethingnewboutique.com.

CHAPTER 9

SILHOUETTES, SHAPES, AND STYLES: HOW TO KNOW WHICH DRESS WILL FIT YOU BEST

As we've discussed so far in this book, the search for your wedding gown can be an overwhelming experience if you're not sure what to look for. Your choice will be much easier when you know the four silhouettes of wedding gowns and which one will look most flattering on your figure. Wearing the right cut of gown for your body type can draw attention to your best features and minimize those about which you're concerned.

The four silhouettes (ball gown, fit and flare, A-line, and sheath) all create varying visual effects on different body types. If you haven't tried on wedding dresses before, it is recommended that you try on at least one dress in each silhouette. This will allow you to see which cut best complements the look and feel you are trying to evoke at your wedding.

The Ball Gown:
The ball gown has a form-fitting bodice with a full skirt. It is the most traditional of all wedding gowns. Ball gowns can have several types of waistlines. These include:
- *Basque* – features a fitted bodice with an elongated triangle beneath and at the front and center of the waistline. This style diminishes the width of the dress at the waist.
- *Natural* – waistlines for this dress are between the hip and the ribcage
- *Asymmetrical* – features a change in waist height from one side of the dress to the other

- *Dropped* – falls several inches below the natural waistline. This style of dress elongates the torso.

The Fit and Flare:
The **fit and flare** is fitted to the body and flares out around your hip area. Versions of this include mermaid and trumpet. This style shows your curves and gives you a nice hourglass shape while still allowing you to have a full skirt and bridal feel to your gown.

A-Line:
A-line gowns (sometimes referred to as Princess Cut) have an A-shape, created by vertical seams running from the shoulders to a flared skirt. They are characterized by their "narrow at the top, wider at the bottom" shape. This style of gown is designed to elongate the lines of the body, adding a classic elegance and an illusion of length. This dress doesn't have a defined waistline. It fits through the torso and then flares out from the waist.

The Sheath:
The sheath is a form fitting dress that closely follows the line of the body. The skirt has either a slit in the front, side, back of the dress or can flare out into a trumpet or fishtail style to make walking easier.

How Silhouettes Look on Different Figures:
Here are several suggestions for consideration when trying on these silhouettes based on your body type. Remember these are generalized recommendations, and you will still want to try on the different styles to find out what fits you best and what you *feel* prettiest in. Body shapes can vary tremendously and there is no "one size fits all" approach. Talk with your bridal consultant about what fits best for you.

Hour Glass Figure (small waist, full hips and bust):
Things to Consider: A-line cut gown with a v-neck or scoop neck is flattering.
Things to Avoid: Sheath silhouette may make your figure look disproportional.

Short-Waisted and Petite:
Things to Consider: An A-line cut elongates a short waist and lengthens the torso.
Things to Avoid: A sheath will make your short waist more obvious.

Long Waist:
Things to Consider: A basque waist ball gown will give you the appearance of a shorter waistline.
Things to Avoid: An A-line cut will elongate you and make your long waist more obvious.

Boxy (undefined waistline – the line from your shoulders to your hips is straight)
Things to Consider: An empire waist gown will de-emphasize your waistline and give you a long, thinning look. Horizontal detailing will draw the eye across the body and combat vertical body lines. Also, oversized shoulders and sleeves will add width to your top and shape to your overall appearance.
Things to Avoid: A sheath will draw too much attention to your middle.

Pear Shaped (smaller on top, heavier on the bottom):
Things to Consider: Choose a gown that will draw attention to the upper half of your body. The silhouette isn't quite as important as the neckline you select. An off the shoulder neckline will flatter your shoulders and chest while drawing focus away from your hips.
Things to Avoid: A sheath will be unflattering. The neckline is important here – but avoid a V-neck that draws the eyes down.

Curvy:
Things to Consider: The ball gown is full and will hide many figure problems in the lower areas. Minimize a thick waist with an empire waistline. An A-line cut will flatter practically any figure.
Things to Avoid: A sheath will make you look heavier than you are.

Full Bust:

Things to Consider: A full bust is flattered in an off-the-shoulder gown or v-neckline with minimal detailing.

Small Bust:

Things to Consider: A small bust looks larger when accentuated with intricate details and on-the-shoulder necklines (like the bateau neckline).

Chapter 10

3 BIG Fallacies that Prevent Brides from Getting the Dress They Want

As a recently engaged bride, you have likely been exposed to a lot of information that will help you plan the perfect wedding. You have likely shopped at several stores and found a dress or two that you've really liked. You may also have brought several people with you to help you look for your dress. Over the years, we've talked with a lot of brides about the BIG fallacies that prevent them from getting the dress they want and the BIG SECRET they wish that someone else had told them before they went out shopping for their dress.

Our goal in sharing these fallacies and the big secret with you is to help say yes to your dress with confidence and excitement once you find them. The three big fallacies about wedding dress shopping are:

Fallacy #1: You shouldn't buy the first dress you try on at the first store you've visited.
While it is a good idea to look to ensure that you make the best choice (it is your wedding after all), it is a fallacy to believe that you can't buy a dress you love at the first store you've visited. After all, you have great taste and are going to pick beautiful dresses from any store that you go to. A large percentage of brides end up buying the first dress they try on for this reason. Their eye is drawn to a dress they *really* love and they end up getting that first dress they tried on from. Those brides who are indecisive usually come back and end up buying that dress (after they've spent time and money on gasoline by driving all over that they could have

easily saved by trusting their instincts and getting the dress they loved when they first tried it on). At our store, we even have a special incentive for decisive brides who buy on their first visit. If you choose not to get your dress on your first visit, we really hope you'll return and get the dress you fell in love with on your first visit. Trust your instincts. You may not find your dress at the first store you go to; but if you do, don't hesitate to begin enjoying the euphoric feeling you'll have knowing that you have *that* part of your wedding all taken care of.

Fallacy #2: If it is meant to be, it won't be sold before I come back.

It is easy to get caught up in the notion of fate and that things happen for a reason. The opposite is also true. Sometimes things happen for no reason at all and for reasons that can't be explained. When you find your dress, it is best to decide to get it then, instead of letting another bride and her mother decide for you. At our store, we dress thousands of brides each year. We are busy and on multiple occasions we've seen brides who have trusted fate wake up to the realization that the dress they loved most had been sold. They cried, pleaded and begged for us to help them get another dress in, but many times it just isn't possible. The question you have to ask yourself is this: If you've found your dress, why would you let another bride and her mother tell you what you will or won't be wearing your wedding day? Isn't that a decision you'd rather make? Believe me, you don't want to return to a store you've been to hoping your dress is still there and leaving crushed that it has already been sold. We've seen that happen on too many occasions and we don't want to see it happen to you. When you find your dress, take control. Don't let the dress of your dreams slip through your fingers and let someone else make the decision for you. You've done the hard work and found your dress. Go ahead and get the dress you love and you'll be absolutely ecstatic leaving the store that no one can take the dress you've found away from you. On top of that, you'll save money by buying your dress on your first visit. You can use that savings for something else that you're planning for your wedding. Don't let the myth of fate determine the consequences of your decisions for you. You decided to marry your best friend and you should also decide to get the dress you love (not let someone else make that decision for you).

Fallacy #3: My mom has to approve of my dress before I buy it. Many brides feel this way because they want to have the approval of the most important woman in their lives. We hope all brides have such a wonderful relationship with their mother.

If your mother wasn't able to come with you when you found your dress, take heart. You're not alone. Keep in mind: 1) It is very likely and probable that the dress you've fallen in love with is sold before your mother has a chance to see it on you (this has happened more times than we care to count and every situation has been devastating to both the mom and daughter who have pleaded to order or get in the dress) and 2) the First Visit Advantage Program savings will be forfeited if you choose not to put some money down on your dress to hold it until your mother can see it.

Many brides find the dress, decide to give their mom a call, and she is so supportive of her daughter finding the one and getting the savings from the first visit advantage program. We want your mom to feel included, so we highly recommend that she come to your next appointment and look for ways to accessorize your dress with you and participate in next steps.

The biggest fallacy of all is when brides believe they can't get a dress because if their mother doesn't like it, she won't be happy. Remember, it is your wedding day and you chose the man you will spend the rest of your life with. She'll also respect and value your decision to get the dress you love and that you'll wear when you stand in front of the man you love to declare your vows to one another.

Often brides worry about this because their mother may be paying for the dress. If your mother is paying for the dress of course you want her to see the dress *you've* chosen. However, one of the saddest things we have ever seen here at our store happened recently when the bride fell in love with the dress she chose and someone else in her shopping party tried to talk her out of that dress. They accepted your choice for a fiancé and since you are the one who will be declaring your love to him, shouldn't you ultimately choose which dress you'll be wearing when you make that commitment? The worst thing that could happen is if you choose to leave any bridal store with your head hanging low because you are so disappointed that someone else didn't approve of your choice. Don't let this happen to you. Be decisive and get what you want. You deserve nothing less.

The BIG SECRET that brides have told us time and time again that makes their lives so much easier is to only bring one or two other trusted individuals with them when they go shopping. This prevents unnecessary confusion or drama. After all, you want their input, not their vicarious choice of what they would wear if they were getting married. Your big day is all about you and accordingly you should get the dress you want. Don't start off your married life by putting yourself in a situation that may have unnecessary drama AND most importantly affect your future relationships with those friends and family members. As we mentioned in Chapter 8, it is a good idea to limit what and who you bring with you to your appointment so you aren't overwhelmed and so you don't leave frustrated.

We sincerely hope this chapter has been helpful to you to prevent you any unnecessary stress or worry about what you should do to get the dress you love. Everyone at Something New Boutique is excited to work with you when you come in and we can't wait to and get the dress you love. We'll see you soon!

CHAPTER 11

UNDERNEATH IT ALL: WHY THE PROPER FOUNDATION WILL AFFECT THE WAY YOU LOOK AND FEEL ON YOUR WEDDING DAY

Once you have your dress, here are some important considerations about the proper foundation you will wear underneath your gown. Almost as important as the dress itself, the undergarments you wear will support the gown, help you accentuate your best features and hide any distractions that you don't want to think about or have others see. In other words, the proper foundation can turn a "so-so" dress into a "so-fabulous" dress!

Now that you have your dress, you'll want to schedule an appointment with a seamstress who can help you shape and sculpt your gown to your body. Be sure to take your slip, shoes and bra with you to your fitting, as this will help your seamstress ensure that your dress fits perfectly to you.

BUILT-IN BRA or BUSTIER:
Many gowns, especially ones with full-embodied corseting have built-in bras. If not, we sell bustiers at our store that can help you look even better in your dress. In fact, at the end of this chapter, we've included a special offer for a bustier that you can redeem when you come back into the store. The goal is that with your bra or bustier that you do not feel that the dress is moving away from your bust when it is zipped, buttoned or laced up so that you don't feel like you need to pull the bodice up. Internal boning will support the bodice of your dress as well as the bust line and should sit firmly on your waist. Because the size of your dress was

probably determined from the average size, unless you have a bra cup size of a DD, you will notice some gaping in the bust area. If this occurs, don't distress! No, your dress was not ordered in the wrong size, it just accounted for all your measurements as a whole, rather than just one measurement (a smaller bust related to the waist measurement). Wedding gowns manufacturers need to account for the biggest bust size possible in each given size standard because you cannot generally add fabric to the dress, but it's much easier to take the dress in.

BRA CUPS:
If you are not sure, your bridal consultant or seamstress can determine the best way to help your dress fit you correctly. If the dress if fully corseted with adequate internal stays (boning sewn into the lining of the bodice of the dress) you may not need a separate bra, but instead, bra cups. Bra cups are sold in pairs with or without silicone gel inserted in the bra cup. Bra cups are usually sewn into the dress by your seamstress. Bra cups are hidden in the bodice of the dress and will not show, even with extreme movement. Bra cups are usually desirable for bra cup sizes of A-B-C-D. Also, bra cups work well if your "girls" are two different sizes. Bra cups can also be used to insert in regular bras for additional cleavage or for help post-mastectomy. Bra cups are also good at filling out the shape of a bodice when you don't necessarily need or want a bigger cup size. The most common alteration, besides a hem to the bottom of the dress, is the bust alteration. Often the best, simplest and least expensive fix to fitting the bust area is having the seamstress sew in a pair of bra cups and taking in the side seams just under the arms. Bra cups and under-the-arm alterations are the best way to prevent you from feeling like you need to pull your dress bodice up during the event.

SEPARATE BRA OR BUSTIER:
A bra or bustier is necessary if you do not feel that your gown has enough internal support to hold your bust up even with the support of bra cups. Evidence of needing a bustier is sometimes manifested by the presence of a deep crease underneath the bust

line when you are standing up straight (with good posture!) or if you feel like your breasts are sagging. If you feel like you need to pull the bodice of your dress up, or if it feels like the dress if dropping, you need additional support. The phrase "you get what you pay for" strongly applies when buying a bra/bustier. Keep that in mind when trying on different styles and sizes. If you have a cup size larger than a D, you probably cannot get away with bra cups, so plan for a good bra in your bridal gown budget. If proper bust/bra support does not resolve the crease under the bustline you might want to consider putting straps on your dress that will usually solve the problem and give you additional bodice support. Spaghetti straps almost always come included your strapless dress. They are not sewn on, but come separately to use or not use at your discretion. If you are not sure, ask your bridal consultant. Simple spaghetti straps are an easy way to secure the bustline for an absolute sure fix and an additional point of support.

It stands to reason that if you are wearing a strapless dress, you should buy a strapless bra. Halter bras, may or may not work with a halter dress. Your seamstress or your bridal consultant at Something New Boutique can recommend one to you. Do not be tempted to wear the clear straps that sometime come with a strapless bra or bustier. The clear straps will show indentation on your shoulders in your pictures. When buying a bra for your wedding dress, it is necessary to be sized professionally.

Make sure that the bra doesn't show, especially when raising your arms. Another option is a stick-on bra. Some brides don't like these as much as bra cups, but for some dresses it works perfectly. Use a stick-on bra if bra cups won't stay in place and a strapless bra shows. Stick-on bras are best used with deep cut "V" neck dresses made with flowy or clingy fabric that moves too much to keep sew-in cups in place. Newer version of the stick-on bra have self-stick adhesive, are made of silicone and are nude in color for a more natural look.

A bustier differs from a bra by supporting not only the breasts but extending down to the waist, and sometimes hips, with various degrees of compression. When wearing a bustier, the ribcage is supporting the dress rather than just the breasts. Bustiers come in different lengths, a shorter version extending only a few inches below the bust line and having a regular bra closure in the back to the longest version, sometimes called a "long-line". A "long-line" bustier can extend to and even over the hips and usually contains "stays" or plastic boning which helps considerably in slimming the waistline. If your usual cup size is larger than a D, consider using a bustier that has boning built into the cups as well as the length of the bustier.

The best way to shop for a bra or a bustier is after you have purchased and received your dress. Decide what you are trying to accomplish with the bustier. Do you need to support your breasts? Do you want to "enhance" your bust? Would you like your waist to appear smaller? Do you need your torso to be smaller to fit into the dress that you ordered a size too small because you thought you would lose weight or didn't believe the bridal consultant when she told you your size...? Do you want something with minimal support that will look sexy underneath the dress (for the party that will take place after the wedding reception!)? Keep all these things in mind when shopping for the bustier.

Besides getting the proper fit, an important thing to think about when trying on a bustier, is making sure that it doesn't show. Your seamstress can usually easily solve any small edges peeking out of the top of your dress. Your seamstress can also shorten a long-line bustier if the stays are extending too far down your torso. For wedding gowns with minimal support, your seamstress might want to sew the actual bustier into the bodice of your gown. This type of alteration usually prevents the bustier from showing and gives the gown a better fit. When scrutinizing a bustier, also make sure that it doesn't show through the fabric of the dress in weird bumps created by the stays on the bustier. Be careful buying a bustier with lace, bows and buttons as those types of embellishments might also show through the gown as awkward looking lumps. Other things to watch for (or watch-OUT for) would be buying a bustier that fits too tight. If you are wearing a strapless dress, a too-tight bustier can push the skin folds up in the back area creating the dreaded "back fat". Sometimes "back fat" can be smoothed out by pushing the skin gently back into the bustier, but most often not.

We've found that even the most ambitious bustier will not take you down more than 1 size. The only product that can truly get you down more than one size is a French corset. This product is worn with your regular bra and wraps around your middle. Depending on your generation, think Scarlet O'Hara in *Gone With The Wind* or Keira Knightly in *Pirates of the Caribbean*. The back is open and laces up the entire length. You will not be able to put on this product without help of a very, very, very, good friend. It is possible to lose several inches in your middle with a French corset but what you loose in inches will be sacrificed in comfort (and possibly health and safety!). Because this product has stays running up and down and all around, there is a possibility of bumps showing. In our professional opinion, it is much better to buy your dress in a bigger size than to try to torture yourself by wearing a French corset!

SPANX!
Out with the girdle, in with the SPANX! If the story behind the creation of Spanx® doesn't inspire you, the names of the products will. Names like Power Panties, Higher Power, and High-Falutin' Footless will make you chuckle as you wiggle your way into Sara Blakely's revolutionary product. Inspired by the lack of practical products, designer Sara Blakely hand-peddled her homemade product into department stores until someone finally took her seriously. Everyone was sold—including Oprah Winfrey, who featured the product on her show and turned the word Spanx® into a household name (or at least the female side of the house). There are a few copycat brands, but for a few dollars more the

quality of the Spanx® product should earn your purchase. Spanx® and similar products are a special type of underwear that is worn instead of typical panties. These products are designed to prevent "panty-lines"and smooth out the area from below the bra-line down to the knees, depending on which product you prefer. Spanx® type products do not have stays of any kind so there is no chance that they will show through any type of fabric. Spanx® and Spanx®-type products range in use from simply preventing "lines" to varying amounts of compression. Some products have a built in bra and can be worn as an "all-in-one" type of garment. These products also come with built-in pantyhose if you do not want to show bare legs. Wear these under flowy or clingy gowns—shapely support and no lines!

SLIP or PETTICOAT:

You may not think you need this, but you really do! Worn at the natural waist (not on your hips), the petticoat creates fullness in the bottom of your bridal gown. If your gown's skirt is an A-Line or ball gown it probably already has some sort of crinoline (crunchy netting) sewn into the lining of the skirt. This is all well and good, but the problem is that because the crinoline is sewn into the dress and is not a separate piece, the netting will not prevent itself from getting caught between your legs while you walk (horrors!). A separate petticoat, sometimes called a crinoline, will keep the underskirt of your dress where it is suppose to be, which is NOT between you legs. Also, by wearing the appropriate fullness petticoat, you will properly show-off the beautiful fabric and shape of the skirt while highlighting any ornamentation on the dress. Also, a fuller petticoat can sometimes raise the bottom of the dress and do away with the need for a hem.

Petticoats come in various degrees of fullness. A ball gown skirt is meant to be very full. Buy a petticoat that will accommodate the necessary fullness. Play with different sizes of fullness when choosing your wedding dress. One of our brides used a semi-full petticoat when trying on her favorite dress. The dress was "okay" until we put on a fuller petticoat. The fuller skirt created a simple drama that made the dress spectacular! Remember that a full skirt will make your waist look smaller. New mermaid slips are now available and are wonderful at accentuating the curves of a mermaid dress. Sheath-style dresses might not benefit from a petticoat, but from its cousin, the slip. Slips will prevent the dress from being see-through and slips also help prevent your wedding dress from sticking to your legs. The ideal petticoat or slip will have an elastic band around the top or will be ordered according to your waist measurement Some petticoats can even be ordered with custom lengths in mind for brides that are shorter in stature. Be careful when using a petticoat with a drawstring enclosure, sometimes these can show through.

If you are wearing a full-skirted dress and your wedding is going to be in a warmer climate, you might want to investigate a hoop style petticoat. "Hoop skirts", as they are sometimes called, contain flexible plastic "hoops" sewn into the fabric, circling the perimeter of the petticoat. Hoop versions come in different styles and sizes (fullness). The fullness is created by size of the perimeter of the hoops instead of netting. Without netting, your legs will have nothing touching them and will only have openness creating room for air to circulate. Also, the hoops prevent the layers of netting, which although lightweight, still create bulk and hold in warmth.

Let your bridal consultant help you determine which kind of petticoat you will need for your dress. Your bridal consultant has seen all kinds of fit both outside and underneath the dresses. You will be amazed at what a difference the right petticoat will make!

Once you have chosen the perfect undergarments and shoes, do NOT forget to bring them to your alteration appointments. Your seamstress *will* reschedule your appointment if you don't have them with you. There is no way that your professional seamstress is going to spend hours pinning, basting, adjusting and sewing a bridal hem using an "approximate" heel height. Pinning the hem involves more than just heel height; your posture when standing in the shoes must be taken in consideration also.

We hope this chapter has been helpful to you to know of the important aspects of everything you will wear under your dress. If you have purchased your dress at Something New Boutique, we have a coupon with savings for your slip or bustier. Simply call to schedule an appointment and we will help you find the perfect solution for your dress. We look forward to helping you find the perfect undergarments to make the fit of your dress even more amazing!

Chapter 12

Tips and Guidelines to Avoid Wedding Day Disasters

So, you have spent the last few months preparing for one of the biggest days of your life, and in some cases the last couple of years. You have gone through every little detail from the color of the dessert napkins to which tux will look best next to you and your bridesmaids. Your venue was carefully chosen, and you fought over who sits at which table at the reception, because let's face it, your crazy uncle shouldn't be sitting at table number five with your nice friend from college. Every element of your wedding day has been accounted for. But what most brides do not spend months planning are the "what-if" scenarios.

One of the most important days of your life is full of those carefully planned details, and the last thing that any bride wants is for months of plans to unravel. Now, before we dive in with how to deal with possible emergencies take into account that any number of things can go wrong. However, focus on the big ones. This is a "choose your battle" event.

Delegating is the key to overcoming wedding day disasters. You don't have to fix all the situations that take place at the wedding you just have to have people around you that are willing to step up and make things right. In the case of the partying guest or relative, don't go near them as you risk too much with a white dress and perfect hair. Find someone to monitor them and get back to the moment you were caught up in.

This is just one scenario in which you can easily control the outcome. Now, let's talk about those small emergencies that no one really anticipates, but can be fixed if prepared for properly.

Your wedding gown is likely one of the first things that you picked out. It is said, "Groom, wedding date, dress, venue, and everything after are just details." Your gown is one of the most important parts of your day. Every detail matters because you have spent so long working on them, but let's be honest: people are there to see you get married to the love of your life and most people will not remember details of the wedding. Some grooms don't even recall what color the bridesmaid dresses were! He will, however, remember you walking down that aisle toward him in the perfect wedding gown.

These are a few emergencies that can be anticipated and prepared for. A spot on the dress is a common emergency. Whether you get a spot before the ceremony or during the reception, it can be dealt with. Make sure that you have on hand: baby wipes, club soda, cheese cloth, a hair dryer, hair spray, a Tide Stain Stick, and white chalk if you have a silk dress.

Say that you get a makeup stain on your dress. Take the baby wipe and gently blot only the area of the stain to get it out. Do not use soap and water because this will make the stain more noticeable. Use the hair dryer once it is out to dry it quickly. If mascara is the culprit, use the cheesecloth and a little water, same procedure. If you get ink on your dress, you can actually use hairspray to lightly blot it out really easily. Red wine can be blotted gently with the club soda. Don't rub, just blot until it comes out. Now, if your dress is silk, do not try to rub, wipe, or wash anything out. You simply need to take white chalk and lightly cover the stain. Silk is such a delicate fabric, that getting it wet or trying to clean it can damage it permanently.

If your dress has a snag in it, the best thing you can do is simply let it go. Pulling on it will only make it worse, and chances of anyone seeing it are slim. If someone does happen to see the snag and says something to you, don't pounce. Just smile and thank them for coming then move on to other guests.

A common problem brides face comes with strapless gowns. How often do you see girls tugging at their strapless dress trying to keep it from falling down? We have had many brides and mothers bring this concern up while wedding dress shopping. Here is what we tell them: "First of all, most of it is mental. Your dress will not fall down. The security of straps or sleeves that you are used to is gone, so it is only natural that you will want to make sure that nothing is going to fall. However, you should also feel secure in your dress. Make sure that you get a dress with built-in boning and bra. A lot of cheaper gowns do not have this and require that you buy the long-line bra instead. With a built in bra, the dress sits perfectly where it should on your waist and will not move." You also need to make sure that you get the right size. If your dress is too small, then the cups of the dress will pucker out so that they aren't flush against your skin. If the dress is too large, then it will feel like it is going to slip. Something to bring with you just in case is double-sided tape, or fashion tape. If you place this on the inside of the dress under the arms then the dress will stay in place a lot better.

Ultimately, the best thing you can do for that assured security is to buy a gown that is made with the built in bra.

The last thing that you need to make sure that you have for a wedding gown emergency is a needle and thread, and make sure the thread matches the color of the dress. Buttons and beads can come off, which is an easy fix. We recently heard a story of a wedding coordinator having to sew the bride into her wedding gown twenty minutes before the wedding!

Since your wedding day is a tapestry of a crazy amount of details, expect other things to go wrong. Here are a few cases of wedding day emergencies that will help you think ahead and plan for a less stressful day.

Think about the color of your wedding cake icing. We had a

friend use dark purple icing on her wedding cupcakes. While it was beautiful, she did not anticipate her groom smashing the cupcake in her face- all fun and games until the bride has a big purple stain on her face. So, if you want a dark color for your icing, either agree to not smash the cake in each others' face or have a few cupcakes in a different lighter color. Now keep in mind that sometimes a guy will promise not to smash it in your face, but then he gets caught up in the fun of the moment and does it anyway. Just saying.

Every bride can attest to the frustration of having guests confirm their reservation at the reception and not show up. On the flip side, most brides can also agree that guests who did not RSVP or even said that they were not coming, and show up are just as frustrating. An easy way to prepare for this fun surprise is to have a few extra chairs set throughout the reception hall. Chances are that some people who said that they were coming will not, which will balance out any of those surprise guests. However, if you prepare for the unexpected, then the worst that can happen is that you have extra seating.

Children are adorable and for some reason it has become a tradition to put little boys in a cute tux and little girls in a small white dress to have them walk down the aisle. When you stop to think about it, how is it that we as adults expect a small child, who is inevitably unpredictable, to walk down the aisle with hundreds of people watching them? However, most brides want their little nephew, niece, or any other cute kid to be a part of their wedding. So here is the truth: a lot of kids, of any age, find that when faced with hundreds of people watching them—all they want is their mom or dad. Or, like the flower girl in our friend's wedding, they may sit down in the middle of the aisle with their flower girl basket and scream at an unbelievable decibel. Kids are wonderful but unpredictable. So, sometimes the best thing to do is have the flower girl or ring bearer walk down the aisle with one of the bridesmaids that they are comfortable with, their mom, or even the bride. We saw a video of a ring bearer who got so scared walking down the aisle, that he ran up and hit the videographer. So, this is a basic fight or flight principle that you need to anticipate.

Another accident to anticipate that involves the ring bearer is his losing the rings. Again, with the ring bearer being a child it may not be the wisest decision to entrust such an important and expensive object with him. A wedding coordinator suggested that the fake rings be put on the ring pillow and give the actual rings to the best man. You don't want to be standing at the altar with no ring to give to your beloved.

These are just a few scenarios that can be anticipated and dealt with before the big day. Like we said before, there are a lot of things that can go wrong. With so many details and so many integrated parts that make up this day, you have to leave a little room for at least a few mishaps. And once you get to the big day keep in mind that the best thing you as the bride can do is relax. What's most important is that you will be married by the end of your big day! You will be walking down the aisle toward the person that you love, and an unforeseen circumstance will not change or even ruin that. So take a deep breath, relax, and enjoy one of the most important and amazing days of your life.

Our Something New Boutique team would really love to see a picture of you in your wedding gown on your special day. Please send us a picture when you get back from your honeymoon! We hope following these tips will help you be at ease on your big day. Don't hesitate to ask if we can help you in any other way as you finalize your preparations for your wedding.

CHAPTER 13

THE PERFECT FIT

One of the most important things about purchasing the perfect wedding gown is being able to have it fit perfectly. There is much more to alterations than pinning and sewing a seam. There is a big difference between basic tailoring and the skills needed for bridal alterations. Unless your gown has been custom made, you will most likely require alterations. Therefore, it is critical that you are measured correctly when purchasing your wedding gown so you can get it as close as possible to the perfect fit before you begin the alterations process.

All eyes will be on you on your special day and the perfect fit is much more important than the size of the gown you are wearing. Try not to stress on the number size. If it is larger than what you normally wear, you must be aware that traditionally bridal gowns run smaller than your street clothes size. There is not a lot any expert seamstress can do if the dress is too small.

You may find that you have fallen in love with 75% of a gown but that there is something missing that would complete the dress for you. Possibly the addition of a cap sleeve, a little more appliqué, extra hem lace or the removal of a flower, waistband, or too much crinoline can turn this dress into your perfect dream gown. An expert seamstress will be able to let you know what can and cannot be done to your dress without ruining the original look of the gown. Many times just removing a layer of crinoline from the skirt of the gown will make the gown lay softer.

The majority of wedding gowns today are strapless and a perfect fit is necessary so you will feel secure in the gown throughout your day. An expert seamstress will know that fitting the gown to the ribcage perfectly will feel better than fitting the bust tightly to keep the dress up. When the bust is fitted too tightly, your skin will bulge over and look unattractive in your pictures, or you will tug at your gown all day. Fitting the rib cage tightly and bust slightly looser allows you to fall into the dress so there isn't any bulge and prevents the need to tug at your dress.

If your perfect gown is an exquisite gown with a beautiful cap sleeve, it is important that the sleeves be attached in the proper place. Cap sleeves that are placed too far to the side will leave you feeling that they are going to fall off your shoulders. Properly attached in front and back they will allow you to move quite freely without feeling that they will slide off. You should not have to use two-sided tape to keep it on your shoulder.

The sides of the gown should be fitted to follow the contour of your body cutting under your bust for good definition. The gown should flow to the waist with a slimming appearance continuing over the hip for that hourglass shape—unless you have chosen a natural-waisted gown. The gown should cut under the bust to a shapely waist usually having a band at the waist and a ball skirt covering the hip.

Having a good rapport with the seamstress is very important so she/he will fit your dress the way you personally feel comfortable in. A lot of times girls are self-conscious of their hips. So, when you're wearing a fit and flare gown the seamstress should fit you a little less snuggly in the hip area so you feel comfortable. Some brides are okay with their hips and want it fitted tightly. Make sure you are comfortable with the alterations being done.

The next part of the alterations on your gown, and a very important part, is the bustle. Since that is the way the gown is worn for the majority of the reception, this point is critical. Bustling is usually done after the wedding ceremony and pictures allow the bride more freedom of movement without dragging the train. Since all brides are not the same height your bustle should be custom made. Your bustle should lift the back of your gown to your hem length.

There are several different types of bustles. A traditional or over bustle is when the train of the gown is pulled up and attached to the top layer of the dress. The determination of where the train is attached is dependent on the style of the skirt. A ball gown silhouette is almost always attached at the waist. A slim A-line, or a fit and flare gown is either attached at the knee or mid thigh depending on the length and shape of the train. Gowns with pick up skirts have to be bustled to follow the basic pattern of the pickups. The second most popular bustle is a French bustle, where the skirt is tucked up under the skirt. There are other ways to pull up the train on your wedding gown and an experienced seamstress can give you several suggestions based on the type of your dress.

CHAPTER 14

TIPS TO PRESERVING YOUR BEAUTIFUL WEDDING GOWN

You have spent many hours and put much thought in the selection of your wedding gown. The gown you've chosen was most likely the most expensive article of clothing you have ever purchased. Even if it was not the most expensive it is likely the most valuable as far as sentiment is concerned. Your gown could be passed down from generation to generation, or remade as a new gown for your future granddaughter, or refashioned as a christening gown for your future great-granddaughter. But, to preserve the memories of your special day and to ensure that your gown will be preserved if you decide to pass it down to future generations, you'll want to follow the steps outlined below. Your gown is a treasured memento, and if cleaned and preserved properly will last for many years to come.

The biggest mistake you could make is to let your dress hang in your closet for months following your wedding. Many well-meaning brides have the best of intentions of preserving their gown, but following the honeymoon, they forget the gown that is in their closet and the weeks turn into months and years before it is thought about again. This procrastination can cause serious damage to your gown and so we invite you to take the time now to purchase a wedding gown preservation kit at Something New Boutique. Then, you'll be able to send your dress to a professional wedding gown preservation company and ensure that your special gown is properly cleaned. Not all dry cleaners are equipped to clean a wedding gown so we recommend that you utilize the service we provide. Fortunately there are many wedding gown preservation companies that specialize in the cleaning and preserving of wedding gowns and we represent them here locally. Since, it is best to preserve the gown within days or weeks of the wedding, please bring in a copy of the coupon you receive with your dress purchase. We can gladly help you send your gown to the best wedding preservation company to ensure the best cleaning and preservation possible.

Many brides are very concerned about what might happen if they spill something on their dress or if it gets dirt or grass stains on it. With the wedding preservation package we offer, you won't have to worry about any of these things and the preservation company will be able to take care of even the most difficult spots or stains. There is no need to worry because they will take care of all of the details and your wedding gown will arrive back at your house within six weeks of you dropping it off at our store.

The best method of cleaning and preserving a wedding gown is through the use of a virgin solvent. Virgin solvent is not only good for the environment but is also good for your wedding gown. Gowns cleaned in virgin solvent will not have a dry clean smell. There is no odor in the gown. Some gowns will require a wet-cleaning method also. Wet cleaning is the best for sugar stains, food stains, and dirty hemlines. The wet cleaning method leaves no chemicals in the gown.

Professional gown cleaners and preservers use both methods depending on the fabric of the gown and the type of cleaning and treatment it will need following your wedding. We highly recommend the wedding gown preservation company we represent. We have had literally hundreds of brides utilize their service and they have all been thrilled with the results. You've invested a great deal in your wedding gown and creating wonderful memories. Now, let us help you clean and preserve your gown.

Some questions you may want to ask a dry cleaner if you are not using a cleaning and preservation service would be:

1. Does the dry cleaner do the work in-house or do they send the gown off premises?
2. Do they use dry-cleaning or wet-cleaning?
3. If the company is dry-cleaning your gown, what type of solvent are they using?
4. How many years of experience does this dry-cleaner have with wedding gowns? Who is doing the cleaning and pressing of their gowns? How experienced is the person that is doing this task?
5. Is this cleaner using virgin solvent to clean the wedding gown?

As the bride, you need to know several things about your wedding gown:
1. What type of fabric is your gown made from?
2. What kind of cleaning does the care label on your gown suggest? If it states dry-clean only, does it also have a symbol for water cleaning also? Please look very carefully; the label may say professional dry-cleaning or professional wet-cleaning recommended.
3. How dirty is your gown? What type of stains does it have (perspiration, wine, food, make-up, etc.)?
4. Is you gown beaded and sequined? Will they need special treatment? Are they sewed on or glued on?

If your gown and/or lining is silk, rayon, or acetate and does not have beads or sequins you should be able to have it cleaned by a dry-cleaners that uses perchloroethylene (perc). For gowns of these fabrics that is a plus, because perc is the best degreaser and this cleaning fluid works great on very dirty hemlines. If your gown is made of these fabrics and does have sequins and beads then the Stoddard formula, Hyrdo-carbon or Greenearth will be the best to use. If you have a heavily beaded gown, it is best to not have your gown treated with percloroethylene as it may melt the beads.

Make sure you point out any stains to your dry-cleaner. Also be sure to point out any spills on the gown, even if they do not show.

Dry-cleaning fluids will not remove sugar stains, so the gown needs to be pre-treated. Professional gown cleaning and preservation companies automatically take your gown through all the necessary steps with out you telling them this information. This is what they do every day and in many cases have been doing for nearly 100 years.

If your gown and lining are polyester (having no beads and sequins or having beads and sequins) wet cleaning is the best method for your gown.

Professional gown preservation companies have common goals that protect your gown from:
- Yellowing
- Permanent creasing
- Mildew
- Mold
- Oxidation spots
- Light
- Dust

Yellowing occurs with age if not pre-treated. The plastic bag you store your wedding gown can be a culprit for a slight discoloration of your gown if it is left in it indefinitely. A plastic bag is designed for short-term storage, but following your wedding it is best to have your dress professionally preserved.

Usually, silk fabrics have a tendency to yellow more than synthetic fabrics such as polyester, rayon and acetate. If your gown has any nylon in it, the likelihood that the gown may yellow goes up since nylon tends to yellow more than other synthetic fabrics. Gowns that are wet-cleaned have an advantage over solvent cleaned gowns when it comes to yellowing. Preserving your gown in an acid-free environment is your best protection against your gown yellowing. All of this is taken care of when you preserve your gown with the professionals we recommend.

Flat storage is recommended for garments when ever possible. However, because of the size of wedding gowns, it is at impractical. Keeping your gown in a breathable environment will protect it best from both mildew and mold growth. When fibers can breathe, mold and mildew does not survive.

Oxidation spots occur when a substance has not been cleaned properly; the spot oxidizes and turns brown. This happens when the gown has not been cleaned properly and the dry-cleaning solvents did not remove all the substances on the gown. Spills from clear soda or wine may not be noticed at the time of the initial cleaning. Unless these spills are pretreated, it is likely they will oxidize over time. The sooner an oxidized stain is caught, the more likely it will be able to be removed.

Keeping your gown covered will protect it from light and dust. Remember that your gown holds so many memories and the picture of you and your gown will be around for over 100 years. Have your gown professionally cleaned and preserved to keep your memories in the best of shape.

We hope this information has been helpful to you as you consider the benefits of preserving your gown. Brides who buy their wedding dress from us are entitled to special coupon off the purchase price of a wedding gown preservation kit. Please call us to redeem the coupon you received so you can take advantage of this great discount.

Section 3:
The Big Day

The Five Biggest Issues that Cause Unnecessary Drama in Your Wedding Planning and How to Avoid Them

Getting engaged is such an exciting and happy time, yet many brides quickly enter treacherous waters as they put all of the details for their weddings together. We've written this chapter to help you identify the BIGGEST issues that can come up with your mother, your future mother-in-law and your fiancé so the little things don't flare up into big things that can escalate into fights and high drama.

Once you're engaged, you would think that everyone would want to work closely with you to help you plan the perfect wedding. However, some brides quickly find that some topics or areas of discussion can create unwanted stress and strain on your closest relationships. To avoid these issues, we've put together a list of the five biggest issues that brides we've worked with have told us brought out the dark side of some members of their wedding party—and how they learned to cope with them on the way to planning their big day.

1. Your ideas versus every one else's ideas.
Shortly after engagement, every bride finds herself thrust into the dynamics of two family relationships. On top of that, you may find that the ideas of what you've thought about and planned for your wedding day may be at the mercy of the opinions of others. One of the saddest things we see is when brides bring their friends to help them pick out a wedding dress and some of their friends dominate

the conversation and suggest their ideas of what will be best for the wedding. Many brides who are in this situation have left our bridal salon with tears in their eyes wondering why others are so adamant about their opinions when it isn't even their wedding.

Drama can escalate quickly when your mother or his mother enters the fray and tries to press their will upon your plans. Again, clarity in communication is key if you are going to avoid seething or screaming of any kind. If drama does start, be sensitive in how you treat one another and try to understand each side. In the end, you may have to make some compromises; but be clear about what it is that you want, since ultimately your opinion *does* count—*a lot*.

If your mother or his mother tries to force their will upon you, it may be helpful to have a conversation where you say something like this: "I respect your opinion greatly. I love you (or your son) and want to understand why this is so important to you. I have my feelings and ideas as well. In the end, I want what will help our families be closer together. If you push your will upon us, we may likely have the wedding you want, but I also know it will likely affect our relationship going forward. My question is this: How will what you want for _____ affect our future relationship?" Being open to understand her feelings can help bring you closer together and may help her see that what you want isn't so hard to understand either. Talking through the tough issues is a great way to deepen the strength of your relationship with your (or his) mother.

2. Who pays for what.
Traditionally, the bride's family pays for the bulk of the expenses of the wedding day. However, if your future mother-in-law keeps adding to the guest list (and they're not paying for any part of the wedding), stress can escalate and sparks can fly. To avoid this, it is wise to have a clear plan of who will be paying for what.
You and your mother should have an honest conversation about what is budgeted for your wedding. The important thing to

remember is that planning for a wedding is really a trial run for many of your future financial dealings. You'll learn a lot about your family, your fiancé's family and your fiancé through this experience. You've all got to sit down and work out the finances for the wedding. Not communicating or assuming that something is okay without getting approval can be a recipe for a shouting match in which neither of you really wants to be involved.

We've written a special report that details more about who should pay for what. If you would like a copy of that special report, please email us at info@somethingnewboutique.com and we'll be happy to send it to you. Then, you'll have a great starting place to talk about who will be paying for what and how it will all be paid for overall.

3. How involved your fiancé is and will be.

One of the biggest complaints we hear from brides is how disappointed they are that their fiancé is not more interested or involved in the process of planning the wedding. The truth is that most men aren't that interested in the color of the table linens or the décor of your wedding. Your fiancé is interested in you! That doesn't mean that you should give up on encouraging him to help you plan out the details. You'll need his encouragement and help.

Most guys don't want to create any conflict between their mother and your mother. As a result, he may often seem uninterested because he doesn't want to get caught up in the middle of any drama.

However, there are likely some things he may be more interested in that other areas of the wedding planning. Have him help you with what he *is* interested in. This means that there are some areas of your wedding planning that you can run by him, but that he won't really want to help you plan out every detail. If this is the case, cut him a little slack. It will go a long way to ensuring a happy and less stressful planning experience for you. In fact, he may even show more interest when he doesn't feel the pressure to plan and do everything since he doesn't want to get between you and the wedding you really want. Our best advice to you is to prioritize what is important to you, negotiate when you feel like you aren't really being heard, but ultimately be willing to compromise so that you can achieve as much family peace as possible. Your ability to work through some of these small issues will be great practice for when the two of you deal with challenging issues that come up once you're married.

4. Where you get married.
Wherever you choose to get married, you will likely have many who will have to travel a far distance to be at the wedding and reception. A lot of drama can escalate here especially if you are both from two different and distant areas.

Some brides find themselves frustrated by a fiancé who isn't interested in their religious traditions. Again, this is a great opportunity to get to know one another. Many of these issues hopefully have already been discussed while you were dating. Some may come out when you start putting all of the details together and you discover that you have different backgrounds and religious traditions. Settling these issues while you are dating and engaged will help you be clear about expectations once you're married.

Many brides and grooms whose families are far apart choose to let one party pick the location for the wedding and the other to pick the location for the reception. This may be a great way for you to both get what you want, but to avoid compromising on what is most important to you.

5. Who comes to the wedding.
When you begin working on your wedding list, conversations about his friends or previous girlfriends will likely come up and should be discussed. If your fiancé wants one of his friends or previous flames to come to your wedding and this causes you

feelings of concern or alarm, you should discuss this before it escalates into something bigger. In addition, there may be a family member that neither one of you really wants to be at the wedding. However, your mother or future mother-in-law may insist that they are there.

If there are concerns with a previous roommate or girlfriend, your fiancé should hear your concerns and worries so you can discuss how to deal with the situation together. Neither of you want unnecessary drama and instead of worrying or stressing about it by yourself, be sure to express your feelings. Hopefully, he will be understanding and desire to work through the issue together. Remember, your wedding isn't more important than your relationship. You don't want or need unnecessary drama in your wedding plans. Discussing how those in both of your pasts will factor into your future relationship is a conversation that you will likely have at some point in your engagement. However, your future is about the two of you, not those who have been in your past.

One of the biggest areas of concern around this is who his groomsmen and your bridesmaids will be. Whoever they are, you should notify them sooner than later and ensure that both have time to plan their tuxes and dresses before time grows short and stress enters the picture. We have beautiful options for tuxes and bridesmaid dresses that we would love to help you with. Please call any member of our staff and we will be happy to set up an interview where we can help you find the perfect tux or bridesmaid colors for your big day. On top of that, either a friendly bridal consultant on our team or one of us would love to help you find your wedding dress, if you haven't found it yet.

While there are other concerns that may come up as you plan your wedding, we hope you'll take the time to sit down and discuss these five important issues with your fiancé and other members of your wedding party soon. It will make a big difference in how successful your wedding plans will go and will definitely make your planning easier and filled with happiness instead of stress.

If there is anything we can do to help you with the attire you will be wearing, please call either one of us or any member of our team at 719-205-9498. We will be delighted to help you find the perfect dress and just the right accessories to match. We are thrilled with your recent engagement and look forward to meeting you and helping make your wedding plans fun and stress-free.

Chapter 16

Dressing Your Bridesmaids

Now that you have your dress, its time to plan a time for you and your bridesmaids to find the perfect dresses to complement yours. To help you in that quest, we've written this chapter so you know some of the best bridesmaid styles that are available and some important considerations for mixing and matching the right styles of dresses for each of your bridesmaids. We'll give you a coupon you can use for each of your bridesmaid dresses when you call to schedule an appointment at our store with each member of your bridesmaid party.

The silhouettes or cuts of bridesmaid dresses are very similar to wedding gowns. However, tea length dresses (just past the knee) are much more popular today than the floor length bridesmaid gowns. Typically, the longer the length of bridesmaid dress, the more formal the event.

One of the most important things for you to consider about finding the perfect bridesmaid dresses are color and fit. With the myriad of options available today, you can pretty much find colors in most any type you could image for your wedding colors. What you must decide is whether to have all of your bridesmaids wear the same color or have several colors that all match and tie together the theme of your wedding.

The other important consideration is to consider the silhouette or cut of each bridesmaid. Let's face it, not all of the special ladies in your life have the same figure. So, it is important to keep their happiness and styling in mind. You want them to feel good about what they're wearing and be comfortable at your wedding, not pulling at the fabric of their dress wishing they could be somewhere else. For this reason, most brides today allow their bridesmaids to wear the same color with different styles of dresses depending on what will be most flattering to their figure. Allowing your bridesmaids to pick their silhouette or style in a certain color is a great way to have everyone feeling fabulous as they celebrate with you on your wedding day and they will love you even more for including them in the process of finding their dress.

There are between forty to sixty colors these dresses can come in depending on the type of fabric of the dress you pick. We encourage you to schedule an appointment at Something New Boutique now so you can find out what will work best for your bridesmaids. That way, you'll also have enough time to order the dresses you want to match and coordinate with everything else at your wedding.

Most bridesmaid dresses are also going to require alterations of some kind since the dresses are made to a certain size and length. Again, be sure you order your dresses quickly so your bridesmaids have enough time to get all of these alterations completed with plenty of time before your wedding.

Typically, bridesmaids pay for their own dress, shoes, any jewelry they wear to accent the dress, and their makeup and hair stylist. You can contribute to some of these costs, but it is a good idea to be up front with what everyone will take care of and by when. We mention this because many times bridesmaid dresses don't get ordered because of one or two bridesmaids who don't understand their obligation to pay for their dress or don't get down to the store quickly enough to get it done.

This can impact the entire bridal party, as dresses aren't ordered from our store until all of the dresses are paid for in your entire party. By planning carefully and coordinating the time and place that your bridesmaids come into the store, we can ensure that everyone has a great experience and that the dresses come in on time (with plenty of time for the alterations to be completed).

We encourage you to come to Something New Boutique to get your bridesmaid dresses. So, please contact us to receive a special coupon to save money on each of your bridesmaid dresses when you all come in together. We can help you find the perfect dresses for each member of your party and most importantly help you save each of your bridesmaids some money.

Don't wait too long to utilize these coupons and select your dresses. With every day you delay, you increase the likelihood that you won't have enough time to get the dresses you *really* want. Please hurry in so you can use them and take advantage of these special savings. To schedule your private bridesmaid appointment, please call us today. We look forward to seeing all of you in our store very soon.

Chapter 17

For Your Mom:
Tips to Help You Have a More Enjoyable Experience as You Find the Perfect Dress for Your Daughter's Wedding

Congratulations! Your little girl is all grown up and is getting married! With that long awaited announcement, you may be feeling some anxiety over what you will wear at your daughter's wedding and wedding reception. In fact, many mothers over the years have privately expressed to us how much drama and stress this announcement has brought to them as they have considered the task of finding the perfect dress. We have written this chapter to ease your mind and share several tips with you that will help you feel less stress about the process of finding the dress you'll wear as you celebrate your daughter's union.

Most of the drama that can come with buying a dress for a special occasion for your daughter's wedding can come from trying to please everyone involved. While you'll want to follow some basic guidelines from your daughter, it is best to remain flexible and strive to find a dress in which you will feel most comfortable.

The key point is that you want something that complements the color scheme of the wedding and that the color you and the groom's mother pick don't clash with each other and/or the bridesmaid dresses. You also want a gown that is formal, but that doesn't upstage your daughter on her big day.

The most important consideration for your gown is timing. Typically, the mother of the groom purchases her dress after you do (although that is not always the case). That said, you'll want to make sure you allow yourself and your daughter's "mother-in-law to be" plenty of time to order your dresses, so you aren't stressed out or worried as the wedding date approaches.

Most of the stress we see from mothers comes from waiting too long and not planning ahead. If you wait to get your dress, it also means that you'll have fewer options when it comes down to finding the perfect matching accessories that will tie everything together. You'll also want to allow time for alterations for the perfect fit. You'll be in a lot of photos on this big day so proper planning will help you feel and look confident and stunning as you pose with your daughter's new extended family. You don't want to be scrounging around all over town weeks before the wedding looking for a dress. You'll end up settling for something you don't really love and there is no reason to do that if you'll just take the time to start looking now and planning ahead. In fact, if you call and schedule an appointment at Something New Boutique, you can receive a coupon to save money on your dress.

The bridal magazines all recommend that you start no later than 6-9 months prior to your daughter's wedding to find your dress. Your daughter likely has some pretty specific ideas about how formal the wedding and reception will be so you'll want to get some feedback from her as to how formal your gown should be. The time of year and the time of the actual wedding will likely also dictate the fabric you choose, the length of the dress and any jacket, cover up or shawl you may need to stay warm.

Traditionally, many mothers have avoided white, ivory, or off-white gown colors. With many celebrities choosing these colors for their recent weddings, it really comes down to what color you feel most comfortable in and that will best match your daughter's overall color scheme. Some of the most popular colors today are champagne and taupe. Continuing changes in fashion have also made black, burgundy, plum, and other pastel colors popular as well.

There are many different styles you can wear for your wedding. Many mothers really like the mix and match skirt and bodice options that are available today. They give a lot of versatility in style and can also change the formality of the dress depending on the formality of your jacket.

Tea-length gowns are also quite popular as well. They are perfect for casual or semi-formal events and offer the added advantage of requiring fewer alterations. The general rule is that the longer the dress, the more formal the event will be.

There are two keys that are critically important to the overall style of your dress. First, don't draw too much attention to yourself. Another less subtle way to say this is to keep yourself classy and covered. Long sleeves are great for fall or winter and have the added benefit of concealing arm issues. The second key is that you'll want to pick a dress you'll feel comfortable in throughout the day.

Once you've selected your dress, it is good etiquette to let the groom's mother know the length and color of your dress so she can pick something in a complementary color and length. The general rule is that the hem length and the sleeve length should be the same. You can also let her know your style so you can avoid overdressing or clashing colors or styles. This will help both of you feel comfortable and can be a great way for you to get to know one another as well.

Another big source of drama that can arise is between you and your daughter over the styling, color, and nature of your dress. Listen to your daughter's requests. After all, it is her big day, not yours. That said, you'll want to compromise by wearing something you'll feel glamorous, stunning, and comfortable in without upstaging your daughter.

At our store, we have a wonderful selection of lovely gowns to suit your taste and to meet the guidelines that your daughter likely has given you. We have dressed literally hundreds of mothers for their weddings. In addition to your great ideas, we encourage you to arrive at Something New with an open mind. Our dedicated team of professionals may be able to recommend a lovely gown that you may not have otherwise considered that you will absolutely love. We get letters from mothers from across the region that have all trusted our recommendations and have been thrilled with the wonderful compliments they have gotten throughout the day of the wedding and the reception. We can't wait to help you find the dress you've been dreaming of and help you have the same experience at your daughter's wedding.

We encourage you to bring in pictures or ideas of what you want and then let us help you find a dress in which you'll feel stunning. We can't wait to meet you and help you find a dress that will turn heads and that you'll be able to celebrate in as you celebrate one of the most meaningful and special days of your daughter's life.

Chapter 18

Your Finishing Touches

The accessories you wear with your wedding gown are critically important for making your transformation into a bride complete. You wouldn't dream of showing up at your wedding without your makeup and hair being done, so don't get married without the proper accessories that match and complete your look. In this chapter, we'll share five tips for finding the perfect veil and tiara.

A veil is one of the final accessories that will make your transformation into a bride complete. It is most often made from varying lengths of tulle (a machine-made crisp, netting like material) and can have a wide assortment of embellishments that adorn its body and edges. Anciently, it was believed that the veil protected the bride from evil spirits. Most brides today wear the veil to top off the perfect dress in a fun, elegant and stunning way. Your veil can have a finished trim with piping (cording) or ribbon or can be unfinished and adorned with crystals, pearls or rhinestones.

Here are five things to do when searching for your veil & tiara:

1. Pick your dress before you pick your accessories. Many veils & tiaras match or have elements that can be found on the dress you choose. Picking accessories before you decide on the dress will most likely confuse you – since you'll be trying to match a style of veil & tiara to a type of dress that may or may not accentuate your best features. It is best to not even try on accessories until you've decided on your dress. Then you can focus on the color and other elements you love about your dress that you want to accentuate with the accessories you choose. The key is to consider what you like first, and then find a veil/headpiece that compliments your gown as close as you can.

2. Pick a veil & tiara that doesn't distract from you or from the dress. If your dress is really ornate and has a lot of beadwork or embroidery, it is best to wear plain or simple accessories so that they don't distract from the dress. A plain dress looks great with a long cathedral length veil or a veil that is adorned with embroidery, lace or beadwork. Also, avoid veils that have really thick ribbons on the edging of the veil because they tend to divert the focus from your face to the veil.

Here are several of the more common lengths of veils for you to consider:

- *Waist-length* – Veils can come with piping (cording), and ribbon along the edge of the veil. A waist length veil falls just below the waistline. Both of these veils have a blusher that is traditionally worn over the face during the ceremony and flipped over the head or removed after the wedding ceremony.
- *Fingertip length* - This veil extends to your outstretched fingertips. It is approximately 45-50 inches in length and can be single or double layered with a blusher front.
- *Waltz or ballet (calf length)* - The veil falls between the knees and the ankle.
- *Cathedral length* - Cathedral veils are typically worn at formal weddings and can be so dramatic that they become the focus of your attire. If your dress is floor length, you may choose a cathedral veil to give the impression of a long train. The veil extends 3 ½ to 5 feet beyond the base of the dress.

Three other types of veils that you may also consider are:

- *Flyaway* – this veil is a shorter veil that just brushes the shoulders. It can be single or double-layered and is most often considered to be a less formal type of veil.
- *Mantilla* – this Spanish styled veil is long and has a lot of lace. It can be made entirely of lace or have heavy lace on the edge of the tulle.
- *Cage* – A cage veil is made up of tulle and lightly drapes around the face or over one eye depending on its placement. They are very elegant and dramatic and can be combined with feathers or flowers for a very distinguished look.

3. Experiment with different placements of the veil, tiara or other accessories in your hair. Most veils have a comb attached so the veil can easily be attached in your hair. Depending on how your hair is styled for the wedding, you may want to place the veil higher or lower on your head. As you examine how the veil looks from every angle, you'll be able to determine what fits you and the dress best. If the veil and tiara seem unstable, you can have your hairdresser secure the veil with bobby pins.

4. Choose a style that best matches your face shape and body type. A good rule of thumb is to pick a length and volume of veil that is the opposite of your face shape and body type. For example, if you have a round face, wear a longer veil that falls along the side of your face to balance and visually narrow your face. If you have an oval or oblong face, wear a poufy veil that will add width. A fluffy, poufy veil can overwhelm a petite bride, while this style of veil can give a taller bride a stronger presence. Try several types of veils on and look at them from every angle to determine what best fits your face and body type. If you aren't sure, ask a friend, family member, or your bridal consultant.

5. Wear a headpiece to complement the veil. A headpiece can complete your look and will most likely contain shapes or patterns of pearls, crystals or beads that will match your dress. Try on several to find one that will best complement your veil placement. If you're not sure, ask your bridal consultant to help you find a specific headpiece that matches your veil and dress. They work with dresses and veils all the time, so they will likely be able to help you find the perfect match.

CHAPTER 19

DRESSING YOUR GROOM AND GROOMSMEN

Now that you have your dress, its time to plan a time for your fiancé and his groomsmen to find the perfect tuxedos so they all look their very best on your big day. To help you in your quest to have each of the men at your wedding look stylish and fashion forward, we've prepared this chapter so you know some of the most important things you'll want to consider before you pick out the perfect tux and accessories for each of them. We also have a special coupon that your groom and each of the groomsmen can use when you call to schedule an appointment at our store for them.

The Right Tuxedo for the Right Body Type

While most tuxedos will fit most body types properly (when sized correctly), it may surprise you that there are some tuxedo styles that are designed to for certain occasions and particular body types. The following are some of the more common styles of tuxedos:

1-button tuxedos – these are the most traditional of all tuxedo styles; they are always appropriate for formal occasions and are the styles that show the most of your vest or cummerbund

2-button tuxedos – these tuxedos are a bit more formal and fashionable than the 1-button tuxedo, but they still have a traditional flair

3-button (or more) tuxedos – This is the most formal of all of the styles of tuxedos.

Here are the different types of lapels:

Peak lapels – the very first tuxedo ever worn was a one-button, peak lapel style; this style is still the most common and traditional

Notch lapels – this style of lapel is the most popular. More than 90 percent of all rentals of tuxedos have a notch lapel.

Shawl collars – a very traditional choice, not the best choice for rounder bodies (as it tends to accentuate that even more)

Style, Theme and Formality

The first thing to consider when picking out attire for the men in your wedding is the style or theme of your wedding day. Will your day be formal, informal, colorful, classic, trendy, or modern? The style of your wedding will play an important role in what you choose for your men's formalwear. If your style is simple and informal or if you are having a beach wedding, choosing a suit for a more relaxed and informal look may be a good way to go. You may also choose a three-piece option with pants or shorts, a shirt and tie to achieve a casual, laid-back look. If you're planning a day that will be traditional and formal, you may choose to wear a full tuxedo complete with a vest or cummerbund and tie. If your look is trendy and modern, you may choose to skip the vest and go for the tie only look. Once you choose which pieces you wish for all the men to wear then you can start to think about color.

Colors

After you decide on the style of your wedding, you'll need to determine the colors the men will wear. This not only includes the color of the vest, tie and pocket square, but the color of the tuxedo itself. You will have plenty of options with the many tuxedo colors available. The most traditional color for tuxedos is basic black. If you are going away from the classic look on your big day there are a number other colors to choose from; chocolate brown, khaki, light or dark gray and navy blue are some great choices if you want a darker color but are trying to get away from black. There are also white and ivory tuxes, many times only the groom will wear one of these to match the bride and the rest of the wedding party will wear a different darker colored tux or suit. You can get very creative with the coordination of your vest, tie and pocket square. Mix and match patterns and colors that compliment each other for added variation and interest. If you've chosen a two-tone bridesmaid dress, you can mix your vest and tie or tie and pocket square with the two different colors for the perfect compliment.

The Jacket

The jacket is a very important piece to your tuxedo look. This decision can sometimes be overwhelming, but it is nice to have options! There are many different factors you should consider when picking out the jacket for your tuxedos. The build of the groom and wedding party should be one major factor on which you base your decision. If the majority of the men in your wedding are tall and slim they will look great in many different styles. For guys who are a bit broader a jacket with a shawl collar which is rounded off and smooth with little detail and one or two buttons that cuts in at the waist will elongate the body. Another thing to keep in mind when thinking about finding formalwear for larger men is that black is very slimming. The peak lapel is a classic look along with the notch lapel these jackets usually have a deep v which can be very flattering for all body types. Variation is created with subtle details such as tone on tone satin bands, chalk striping, pin striping, and tone on tone texture.

Trousers

The trousers for the tuxedo jacket will be determined, somewhat, by the jacket you've selected. If the jacket you've selected has a pattern or details in it, there is—more than likely—a matching trouser to go with it. If you've chosen a solid jacket without pattern, you can usually choose from a flat front or pleated trouser for your wedding party. The front of the trousers is where you will see the difference between pleated and flat front they are just as their names say flat in the front or pleated. The side of the trouser will typically have a satin stripe down the side of it on both legs. You should take into consideration the overall size of your wedding party. In general, flat front trousers are the dominant trend today and for the last decade or more. If your men are more on the athletic side, you could sport a flat front tuxedo. If your men are not very fit and need a little room in their trousers, pleated trouser could be a better choice for your group. In general, the same style and color trousers should be worn throughout the men in the wedding party.

Shirts

Shirts provide another opportunity to add character to your wedding day attire. There are several different shirt styles to choose from. The collar is the most noticeable detail of the shirt that you will have a chance to pick out. There are lay down, banded, and wing-tip collars. When you are choosing which sort of collar you will want, it is important to keep in mind what style of tie you will want the men to wear. A lay down collar will normally accommodate any style of tie, while a banded collar is typically worn with no tie. The wing tip collar looks best with a classic bow tie or string tie. Pleating is also added to some styles of cotton shirts to give a traditional look. The basic colors for shirts are white and ivory, which should be based off the brides wedding dress. You can also choose colored shirts such as pink, blue, black or chocolate, some of which may also have a whisper stripe. Microfiber material is the latest most popular material today providing a very smooth texture and feel and often many color options.

Accessories, Vests and Cummerbunds

Accessories put the finishing touches on your whole wedding day look. The vest, cummerbund, tie, pocket square, studs and cuff links, and shoes not only bring your whole look together but also are also another great way to reflect your own personal style. Vests and cummerbunds can drastically alter the look of your tux. In the past a cummerbund was a staple for all tuxedos, recently, vests have become more popular they seem to be a more flattering way to add color to your tux or just keep the guys looking great when they decide to take off their jackets. Vests come in many different colors and textures and there are even camouflage and tropical prints to choose from. You may choose to have the men in your wedding wear neither a vest nor cummerbund if you are going for a more casual look.

In many cases, the groom wears white or ivory accessories. The vest, tie, and pocket square should match the color of the bridal gown if you decide to go with white or ivory. The groomsmen typically go in the color of the bridesmaid's dresses, but the same pattern as the groom. The ushers of the wedding can vary with an accent color or a neutral color, such as silver. The fathers of the wedding should have a neutral color, like black, to be easily paired up with the moms of the wedding. The patterns and style can all be the same, but the colors can vary according the role of the person in the wedding.

Ties

Ties come in many different styles, patterns, and colors. The different tie styles can really change the look of your formalwear. Bow ties are typically a more classic and formal look, they are often a solid color or black but some of them do come in a textured or patterned fabric. The Windsor tie has become increasingly more popular in recent years; it creates a more modern and slightly more casual look than the bow tie. Windsor ties come in a wide array of patterns, textures, and colors. Some other less common ties that can create very unique looks are the cravat, string, bolo, and cross over ties. The cravat is usually tied in an ascot knot and is a vintage look usually paired with a cut away jacket. The string, crossover, and bolo ties are perfect for a western themed wedding they look great when paired with a dark jean and casual jacket.

Pocket Squares

Pocket squares are a great way to add a splash of color to your tux jacket; they come in many different colors and patterns. Many people match the pocket square with the tie they have chosen, or choose a completely different accent color. Pocket squares can also be folded in different ways; folding techniques range from basic to exotic. Some of the more popular folds are the winged puff, three fold stairs, and the four point crown. Any way you fold them pocket squares will add a little bit of personal flair and color.

Cufflinks and Studs

Cufflinks and studs give your shirt a very polished look. The selection of cuff links varies greatly from a simple black and silver to a show stopping diamond studded accent or a personalized link with an engraved monogram. Again, the style of your wedding should be kept in mind when picking out all accessories.

Shoes
Shoes should be the last things you pick out. You should only pick shoes that match once you have the rest of the tux all figured out. The classic shiny black tux shoe is the most commonly chosen option. Shiny black square toe shoes are becoming increasingly popular. There are many other ways you can go with your shoe selection, there are matte shoes in black and brown, usually these look best with a more casual look such as, a suit, in the corresponding color. If the color you have chosen for your tuxedos is white or ivory then a shiny white or ivory shoe would look best. There are even shiny black sneakers made as a tux shoe for the man who can't live a day with out the comfort of tennis shoes. These days people are getting very creative allowing their groomsmen to wear actual tennis shoes or other matching shoes. In some western themed weddings a cowboy boot is appropriate.

No matter what you choose for all the men in your wedding to wear, try to take into consideration what they will feel comfortable and look great in. Remember you will look back at your pictures from your big day for many years and you want everyone to look their best!

CHAPTER 20

MAKING YOUR WEDDING DAY PERFECT

Your wedding day is the one day in the world when you want everything to go perfect. You've spent months planning your big day and you want it all to go right. To help everything run smoothly, avoid confusion, prevent panic and be absolutely thrilled throughout your day, take some time to think through this wedding day checklist (based on the time you will get married) and enlist the help you'll need to make it all possible. Now you can stop worrying, start scheduling, get organized and be ready to enjoy your big day!

❑ Wake up and eat breakfast. Be sure to have a healthy, high energy breakfast such as cereal, yogurt, fruit, and a bagel with cream cheese to get instant energy. Don't skip meals. You'll need your energy throughout the day and eating well will help you avoid the jitters and nervousness.

❑ Check a weather report to confirm what the day likely has in store. Have a back-up plan if any adjustments need to be made. These plans should be established and discussed with the vendors helping you put together your wedding in advance.

❑ Get some light exercise—it will help you relieve stress and perk up your energy. Strenuous exercise should be minimized or eliminated from your daily routine.

❑ Shower and begin getting ready. Enjoy a relaxing soak in the tub if you prefer. When dressing, put on your undergarments under a robe if your stylist is coming to you or wear a button down shirt if you are traveling to a salon (you can easily take off the button off shirt when your stylist is finished without messing up your hair and makeup). Wear a shirt that is the same color as your dress so you can be sure to get the color scheme for your makeup right.

❏ If you are changing at the hotel, ceremony site or reception site, be sure to bring your pre-packed beauty and emergency bag, favorite play list and speakers and any other necessary items you'll need. If you have forgotten anything, now is the time to have one of your bridesmaids run a quick errand. Have your mother or maid of honor in charge of making sure your dress, veil, and other accessories arrive safely.

❏ Make sure that your maid of honor or other bridesmaid have their assignments to follow up with each of the vendors for transportation needs, flowers, food, cake, and any other day-of arrangements that you have previously made. Have a contact list with the vendor's phone numbers on it and have them help you coordinate the day or have a wedding planner help you with all of the details.

❏ Have your bridesmaids arrive at the wedding site location with their dresses and accessories.

❏ Meet with the stylists and artists you've contracted with to do hair and makeup. Your maid of honor should have her makeup and hair done first. Spend time with each of your bridesmaids as they take turns getting ready. This is your time to laugh, share stories, visit, pack for your honeymoon, or anything else that you and your bridesmaids have worked out in advance.

❏ Groom's mother and sisters who aren't part of the wedding party arrive.

❏ Enjoy a light snack or lunch.

❏ Have your hair and makeup done. Be sure to give the stylist your complete attention. Now is not the time to eat, chat on your cell phone or be involved in distracting conversations with friends or family. Enjoy this time to get ready. Relax. Your makeup and hair will soon be flawless.

❏ Have the bouquets that have been delivered or picked up distributed prior to your pictures being taken.

❑ Have the photographer take pictures of you and your bridesmaids getting ready, looking into the mirror and other candid shots of you interacting with your mother, maid of honor, bridesmaids and other members of the wedding party.

❑ Visit the ladies' room one last time before getting dressed. Let your attendants help you get into your wedding gown, shoes, jewelry and gloves. Delight in how gorgeous you look and feel. Of course if you don't, your attendants will all be there to pour out praise and fuss over you. Enjoy the moment.

❑ If you haven't already done so, sign your marriage license. Your maid of honor can sign as your witness.

❑ Depending on the location and venue of your wedding, gather with members of your wedding party and prepare to make your entrance. You will need to work out the details for how the rest of the processional will take place based on your religious or personal preferences.

❑ The guests take their seats.

❑ Officiant walks down the aisle and takes his/her place.

❑ Groom and best man walk down the aisle and take their places.

❑ Procession music begins.

❑ Your attendants walk down the aisle and you enter with your mother and father and head down the aisle as your dearest friend and soon-to-be husband sees you for the first time and catches his breath.

❑ Enjoy the ceremony together as you exchange vows and make promises to each other.

❑ Let the party begin! Again, enlist the help of your bridesmaids or wedding coordinator to make the reception flow smoothly and enjoy your perfect day!

Congratulations, you've done it! It has been our sincere honor to share these pages with you. We've been in "your shoes" before preparing for our own wedding. We look forward to getting to know you better as you plan your wedding. Please let us and the amazing team at Something New Boutique know how we can help you plan the details for your big day. We look forward to helping you make your wedding day a treasured experience that you'll always remember.

ABOUT THE AUTHORS

Mindi and Jordan Linscombe started Something New Boutique in Colorado Springs, Colorado in 2007. Their store slogan is "Where The Girl Comes Before the Dress." They have helped brides from Colorado and throughout the United States find the perfect wedding dress. In addition to wedding gowns, they offer stunning formal gowns, bridesmaid dresses, mother's gowns, and tuxedos to make any special occasion one that will be treasured and fondly remembered by all. They are the parents of three children.

Heather and Jim Butler have helped thousands of brides find the perfect wedding dress at their retail bridal stores. They love the wedding business and enjoy helping brides have an amazing experience as they find the perfect dress. They are the parents of five children.

www.ingramcontent.com/pod-product-compliance
Lightning Source LLC
Chambersburg PA
CBHW060633290526
45793CB00001B/228